THE DISCONTENTED

Also by Alan Ogden

Romania Revisited,
On the trail of English travellers 1604-1938

Fortresses of Faith,
A pictorial history of the fortified Saxon churches

Revelations of Byzantium,
The monasteries and painted churches of northern Moldavia

Winds of Sorrow,
Travels in and around Transylvania

Moons and Aurochs,
Travel around Romania

The Vagabond and the Princess
Paddy Leigh Fermor in Romania

THE DISCONTENTED
(Les Méscontens)

*Betrayal, Love and War
in Habsburg Hungary*

Alan Ogden

Nine Elms Books

This edition published in 2018 by Nine Elms Books Ltd

An independent imprint of Bene Factum Publishing Ltd

Unit 6B
Clapham North Arts Centre
26-32 Voltaire Road
London SW4 6DH

Email: inquiries@bene-factum.co.uk

www.bene-factum.co.uk

ISBN: 978-1-910533-26-0
e-book 978-1-910533-27-7 The Discontented   Epub

Copyright © Alan Ogden 2005

Protected by copyright under the terms of the International Copyright Union: all rights reserved. Except for fair use in book reviews, no part of this publication may be reproduced in any form or by any means, electronic or mechanical, including photocopying, recording or by any information storage or retrieval system without prior permission in writing from the copyright holder.

The Discontented: Betrayal, Love and War in Habsburg Hungary.

Photographs of the paintings at Sárospatak of Ferenc Rákóczi II, Imre Thököly and Helena Zrinyi are reproduced with the kind permission of the Hungarian National Gallery.

Front cover: 'Rakoczi Ferenc elfogatasa a nagysarosi varban' (The arrest of Ferenc Rákóczi) by Gyula Benczúr, Hungarian National Gallery [1865]

Design and typesetting by Alex Thornton, www.alex22362.com

Printed in the UK

Contents

Acknowledgements vii
A note on names viii
Comparative values of currencies ix
The Principal Players 1664-1735 xi
Chronology of Tumult xvii
Maps
    Hungary in 1568 and adjoining land xxi
    The Battleground xxii
    Rákóczi: The Long Road to Exile xxiii
Chapter One: Prelude to Rebellion 1
Chapter Two: The Magnates' Conspiracy 13
Chapter Three: Imre Thököly and Helena Zrinyi 44
Chapter Four: Ferenc Rákóczi II 65

Sources consulted 103
Locations visited 107

Acknowledgements

Among the many who assisted me in my research, I would like to thank Philip Barker and Kinga Jackus in Budapest, Vladimir Kalsan of Cakovec Castle, Denis Pleic, my interpreter in Croatia, Marta Santarsieri of the Hungarian Cultural Institute in London, Dr Edit Tamas of Sárospatak Castle, Professor Patrick Salmon of the Foreign & Commonwealth Office, Michael Meredith of College Library [Eton] and Chris Daly.

A Note on Names

The political geography of this story can be confusing. After the fall of Buda in 1541, Hungary was divided into three parts. A large central triangle extending well to the north of Budapest and including the Great Plain and the eastern half of Transdanubia as well as the north-central mountains and the southeast part of Transylvania became an integral part of the Ottoman Empire. The narrow northern area—Upper Hungary—and the western provinces including Croatia formed Royal Hungary. Central and northern Transylvania, which had belonged to Hungary since 11th century, became semi-autonomous.

Place names in former Austro-Hungary are always a sensitive issue—Hungarian history books spell them in Hungarian and most of the Austrian, Croatian and Romanian historians likewise tend to use their own spellings. However, the map on which the drama of The Discontented was played out has long since been redrawn, so to simplify the identification of locations, I have spelt place names according to today's national territories, except in the case of important treaties e.g. the Peace of Karlowitz rather than Sremski Karlovci.

Where appropriate, the names of people are spelt in their original form. In the case of the Zrinyi and Frangepán families, I have not used the Croatian spellings of Zrinski and Frankopan since the Hungarian spellings are widely used in historical accounts. But they did indeed consider themselves to be Croatians within Royal Hungary and are honoured today as national heroes by Croatia.

Helena Zrinyi—often referred to as Ilona or Elena—signed herself Helena, so I have kept to her own spelling.

The Hungarian style of address is to refer to people by their surname, followed by their Christian name. I have reversed this in order to conform to common English-speaking practice.

Comparative values of currencies

Trying to convert 18th European currencies into their modern day equivalent values is an inexact process. However, by going through their exchange rates with the British Pound (One Pound in 1700 being the equivalent of £111.24 in 2002), I have arrived at the following very approximate values:

1 Gulden or Forint = 17 Euros 1 Ducat = 84 Euros

1 Livres tournois = 7 Euros

1 Thaler = 22 Euros

The Principle Players

The Conspirators—1664–71

Count Ferenc Nádasdy III, Lord Chief Justice of Hungary and later Palatine of Hungary.

Cardinal György Lippay, Primate of Hungary and Archbishop of Esztergom.

Count István Thököly, a landowner.

Count Ferenc Wesselényi, Palatine of Hungary.

Count Ferenc Rákóczi I, a landowner.

Count Nikolai Zrinyi, Ban of Croatia.

Count Petar Zrinyi, Ban of Croatia and brother of Count Nikolai.

Count "F.K." Frangepán, brother-in-law of Petar Zrinyi.

Count Erasmus von Tattenbach, a nobleman from Graz.

Count Ferenc Bónis, an unrepentant rebel.

Maria Wesselényi, Ferenc's widow.

Zsófia Báthory, widow of György Rákóczi II and mother of Ferenc I.

The Hungarian Leaders of the First Rebellion 1672-94

Count Imre Thököly, outlawed son of István and leader of the First Rebellion.

Countess Helena Zrinyi, daughter of Petar, widow of Ferenc Rákóczi I and wife of Imre Thököly.

Count Mihály Teleki, a Transylvanian soldier and landowner.

Pál Wesselényi, son of Ferenc.

Dániel Absolon, Helena's political secretary.

András Radics, captain of Mukachevo castle.

Mihály Apafi I, Prince of Transylvania.

István Vitnyédy, a lawyer.

The Hungarian Leaders of the Second Rebellion 1703-11

Prince Ferenc Rákóczi II, son of Ferenc I and leader of the Second Rebellion.
Count Miklós Bercsényi, Rákóczi's neighbour and mentor.
Count Simon Forgách, a kuruc general.
Count Ferenc Barkoczy, a kuruc commander.
Counts István and **Mihály Csáky**, kuruc commanders.
Baron Sándor Károlyi, kuruc commander-in-chief.
Colonel, later **General**, **Vak Bottyan**, a valiant kuruc officer.
Brigadier László Ocskay, another valiant kuruc officer.
Count Antal Eszterházy, a kuruc commander.
Count Lorinc Pekry, a kuruc cavalry commander.
Kelemen Mikes, Ferenc Rákóczi II's secretary in exile.
Pál Ráday, kuruc diplomat.
Princess Charlotte-Amalie Hesse-Rheinfels, wife of Ferenc Rákóczi II.
Jozsef and **György Rákóczi**, Ferenc Rákóczi II's sons.
Juliana, Countess of Aspremont, sister of Ferenc Rákóczi II.
Princess Elizabeth Sieniawska, Ferenc Rákóczi II's lover and mentor.

The Habsburgs

The Emperors

Leopold I (1657-1705)
Joseph I (1705-11), elder son of Leopold.
Charles VI (1711-40), younger son of Leopold.

Their advisers

Prince Portia, Grand Chamberlain.
Prince von Lobkowitz, President of the Aulic War Council.
Johann Paul Hocher, Chancellor.

The Principal Players 1664–1735

Christof Abele, Secretary of the Privy Conference.
Count Johann Rottal, a Commissioner of Hungary.
Count Johan Kaspar von Ampringen, a Commissioner of Hungary.
Prince Schwarzenberg, a diplomat.
Count Nostitz-Rieneck, Chancellor of Bohemia.
Count Johann Wenzel Wratislaw, Chancellor of Bohemia and mediator.
Prince Ferdinand Dietrichstein, a Commissioner of Hungary.
Count Miklós Pálffy, Chancellor of Hungary.
Vice-Chancellor Count von Kaunitz, Chancellor and mediator.
Baron Johann Friedrich von Seilern, Chancellor and mediator.
Prince Johann Adam von Liechtenstein, commissioner for Hungary.
Prince Francois-Louis de Salm, General and Grand Chamberlain.
Count Philipp Ludwig Sinzerdorf, Chancellor.
Count Alois Thomas Harrach, Grand Chamberlain.
Prince Pál Eszterházy, Palatine of Hungary.

Their generals
Duke Charles of Lorraine
Prince Louis of Baden Baden ('Turkenlouis')
Prince Eugene of Savoy
General Caprara
General Count Caraffa
General Baron Herbeville
General Count Heister
General Herberstein
General Rabutin de Bussy
General Count Montecucculi
General (János) Pálffy

General (Ernst Rüdiger) Count Starhemberg

Generals von Schlick, Schmidt, von Würben, Spankau, Spork, Vird, (Adam) Zrinyi, (Guido) Starhemberg, and Kopp von Neuding.

Their bishops

Bishop Kollonics

Archbishop Szelepcsényi

Archbishop Széchényi

Their ambassador

Count Caprara, the Imperial Ambassador to the Porte.

The Ottomans

The Sultans

Mehmet IV (1648-87)

Suleyman II (1687-91)

Ahmet II (1691-95)

Mustafa II (1695-1703)

Ahmet III (1703-30)

Mahmut 1 (1730-54)

Their principal Sadrazams

Mehmet Köprülü (1656-61)

Ahmet Köprülü, Mehmet's son and successor (1661-76)

Kara Mustafa (1676-83)

Mustafa Köprülü (1689-91)

Hüssein Köprülü (1697-1702)

Nevsehirli Ibrahim Paşa (1718-30)

The French

Louis XIV, King of France

The Principal Players 1664–1735

His soldiers on secondment to the rebels
Colonel Comte d'Alenduy Boham
Comte de Dampierre
General de la Riviere
Colonel Chassant
Colonel Le Maire
General de la Mothe
Officers Fierville d'Herrissy, Baron Vissenaque, Charriere, d'Absac, Despignon and Norwal.

His ambassadors
Comte Grémonville
Marquis Béthune
Marquis du Héron
Marquis de Sébeville
Duc de Villars
Marquis De Ferriol

His liaison officer to the rebels
Pierre Puchot Comte Des Alleurs, Lieutenant General and envoy to Hungary.

The English and the Dutch

William of Orange, later William III of England.
Queen Anne, his consort and later Queen of England.
The Duke of Marlborough, soldier and architect of Louis XIV's defeat.
The Earl of Sunderland, Marlborough's son-in-law, a diplomat.
Lord (George) Stepney, a diplomat.
Count Adolf Hendrik van Rechteren, a mediator.
Jacob Jan Hamel-Bruynincx, a mediator.

Other players

Peter the Great, Tsar of Russia, architect of modern Russia.
David Corbea, the Tsar's emissary to Rákóczi.
Jan Sobiewski, King of Poland and victor of Vienna.
August the Strong, Elector of Saxony and King of Poland.
Charles XII of Sweden, ally of France.
Pope Clement XI, proponent of the Counter-Reformation.
Max Emanuel von Wittelsbach, Elector of Bavaria and ally of France.

Princes of Transylvania

György Rákóczi II, Prince of Transylvania, father of Ferenc Rákóczi I.
Mihály Apafi II, son of Mihály Apafi I.

Chronology of Tumult

Prelude

- 1526 Ottomans defeat Hungarian King at battle of Mohács.
- 1541 Buda falls to Ottomans.
- 1547 Treaty of Edirne leads to division of Hungary.
- 1593–1606 Thirteen Years War between Habsburgs and Ottomans.
- 1606 Treaties of Vienna and Zsitva-Torok give Transylvania independence.
- 1655 Leopold I crowned King of Hungary.
- 1657–8 Ottoman campaign to suppress György Rákóczi II; Transylvania under Turkish control.

The Magnates' Conspiracy

- 1660 György Rákóczi killed at Oradea.
- 1664 Christian victory at Saint-Gotthard; Peace of Vasvár; death of Nikolai Zrinyi.
- 1665 Beginning of the Magnates Conspiracy in Hungary.
- 1666 Marriage of Ferenc Rákóczi I to Helena Zrinyi.
- 1669 Crete falls to Ottomans.
- 1670 Rebellion in Hungary.
- 1671 Execution of Petar Zrinyi, Ferenc Nádasdy and others.

The First Rebellion

- 1672 Rebellion resumes in Hungary.
- 1673 Imperial governor appointed to rule Hungary.
- 1676 Death of Ferenc Rákóczi I.
- 1678 Teleki hands over command of the kurucs to Thököly.
- 1681 Session of the Hungarian Diet at Sopron; Thököly takes up arms in Hungary.

1682 Marriage of Thököly and Helena Zrinyi; Thököly a vassal of the Porte.

1683–99 Ottoman war against Habsburgs, Venice, Poland and Russia.

1683 Second siege of Vienna by the Turks; Austrian/Polish victory at Kahlenberg.

1684 The Holy League (consisting of the Republic of Venice, the Austrian Empire, and Poland) unites against the Ottomans.

1685 Thököly imprisoned by the Turks; siege of Mukachevo begins in December.

1686 Seizure of Buda by Imperial troops.

1687 Turks defeated at second battle of Mohács; session of the Hungarian Diet at Pressburg at which Joseph I elected king; Caraffa's Presov tribunals; Ottoman army mutinies; Transylvania reunited to Habsburg Hungary (Treaty of Blaj); Joseph I crowned King of Hungary.

1688 Mukachevo surrenders; Helena Zrinyi detained in Vienna; capture of Belgrade by Imperial troops.

1690 Diploma Leopoldinum guarantees liberties to Transylvania; Thököly defeats Imperial forces at Zarnesti; Ottomans retake Belgrade.

1691 Prince Louis defeats the Turks at Novi Slankamen.

1694 Thököly and Helena Zrinyi reunited, then exiled; Ferenc Rákóczi II marries Charlotte-Amalie of Hesse-Rheinfels.

Interlude

1697 Victory of Prince Eugene of Savoy over the Ottomans at Zenta; peasants revolt at Sárospatak and Tokaj.

1699 Signing of the Peace of Karlowitz between the Porte and the Holy League.

1700 Death of Charles II; Louis XIV accepts his will.

1701 Beginning of the War of the Spanish Succession; Rákóczi arrested and escapes to Poland.

Rákóczi's War of Independence

1702 Beginning of the Hungarian war of independence.

1703 Death of Helena Zrinyi; proclamation of Berezhany.

1704 Defeat of the Franco-Bavarian army at Blenheim; Heister defeats rebels at Koronco; Ferenc II Rákóczi becomes Prince of Transylvania; peace negotiations begin between Rákóczi and Vienna through Anglo-Dutch mediators; stalemate at battle of Trnava.

1705 Death of Leopold I and succession of Joseph I as Emperor; death of Thököly; Assembly at Szécsény announces Hungarian Confederation; kurucs defeated at battle of Jibou.

1706 Peace negotiations finally collapse.

1707 The Diet of Onod; Joseph I deselected as King of Hungary.

1708 Heister defeats Rákóczi at the battle of Trencín.

1709 Plague sweeps through Hungary.

1710 Rákóczi defeated at battle of Romhany.

1711 Death of Joseph I; accession of Charles VI; Peace of Szatmár; Ferenc II Rákóczi goes into exile.

Rákóczi in Exile

1711 Ottoman forces defeat the Russians at the battle of Prut.

1713 Peace of Utrecht.

1715–18 Ottoman war against Habsburgs and Venice.

1717 Belgrade falls to Habsburgs.

1718 Treaty of Passarowitz; the Turks cede the Banat of Timisoara.

1720 Rákóczi arrives in Turkey.

1725 Miklós Bercsényi dies at Tekirdağ.

1735 Death of Ferenc Rákóczi at Tekirdag.

1738 Jozsef Rákóczi dies.

1756 György Rákóczi dies in Paris.

1761 Kelemen Mikes dies.

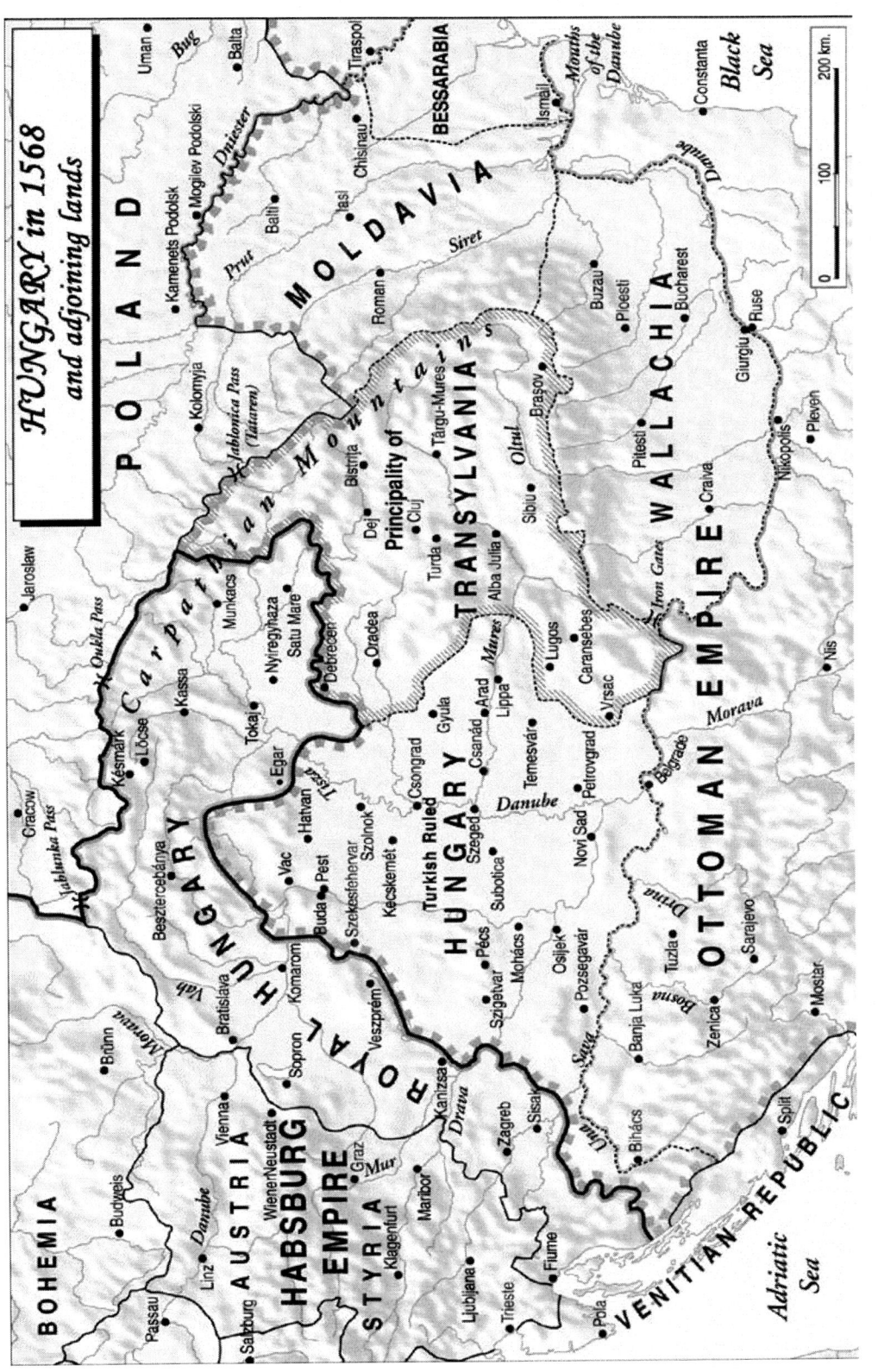

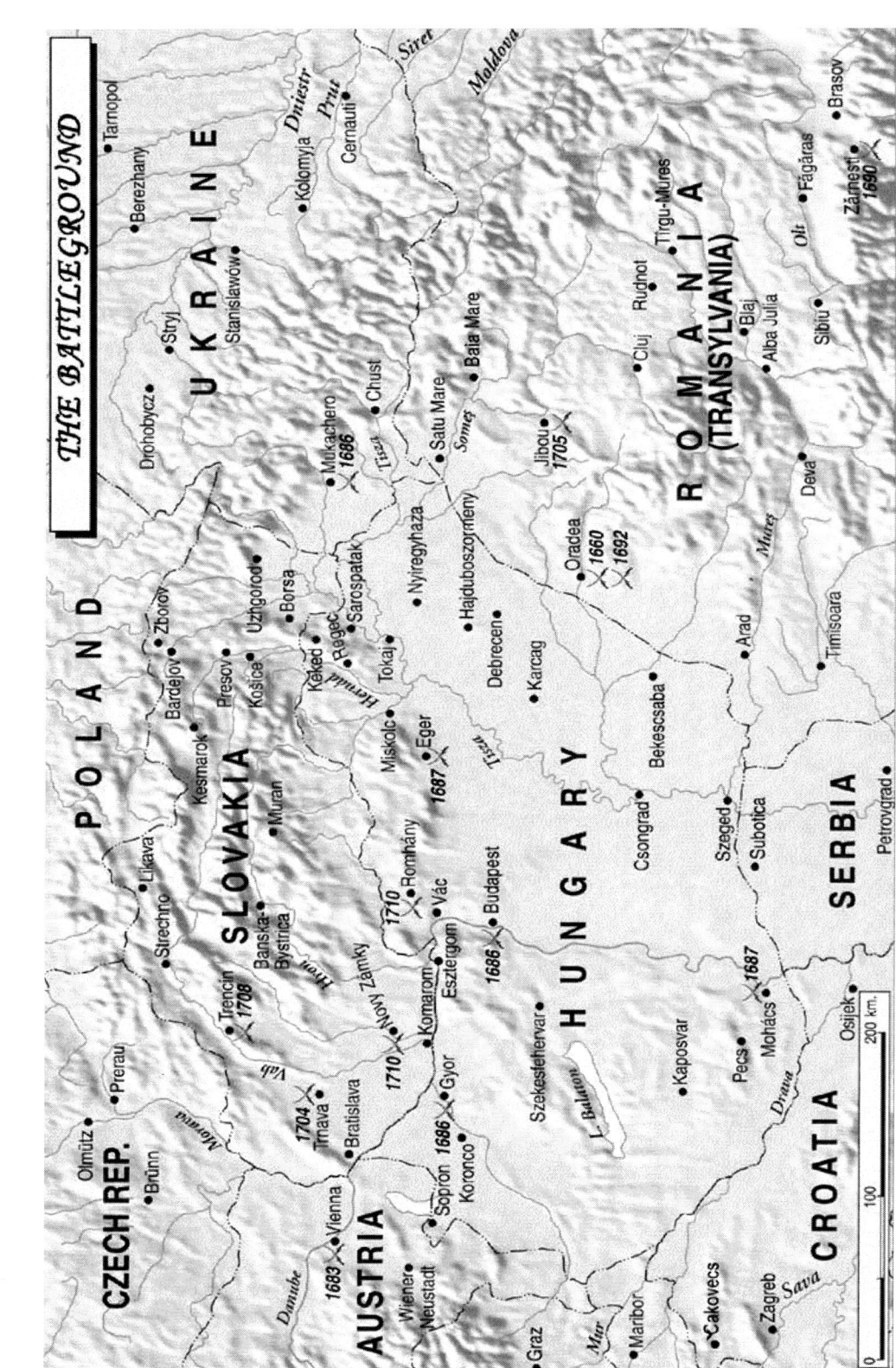

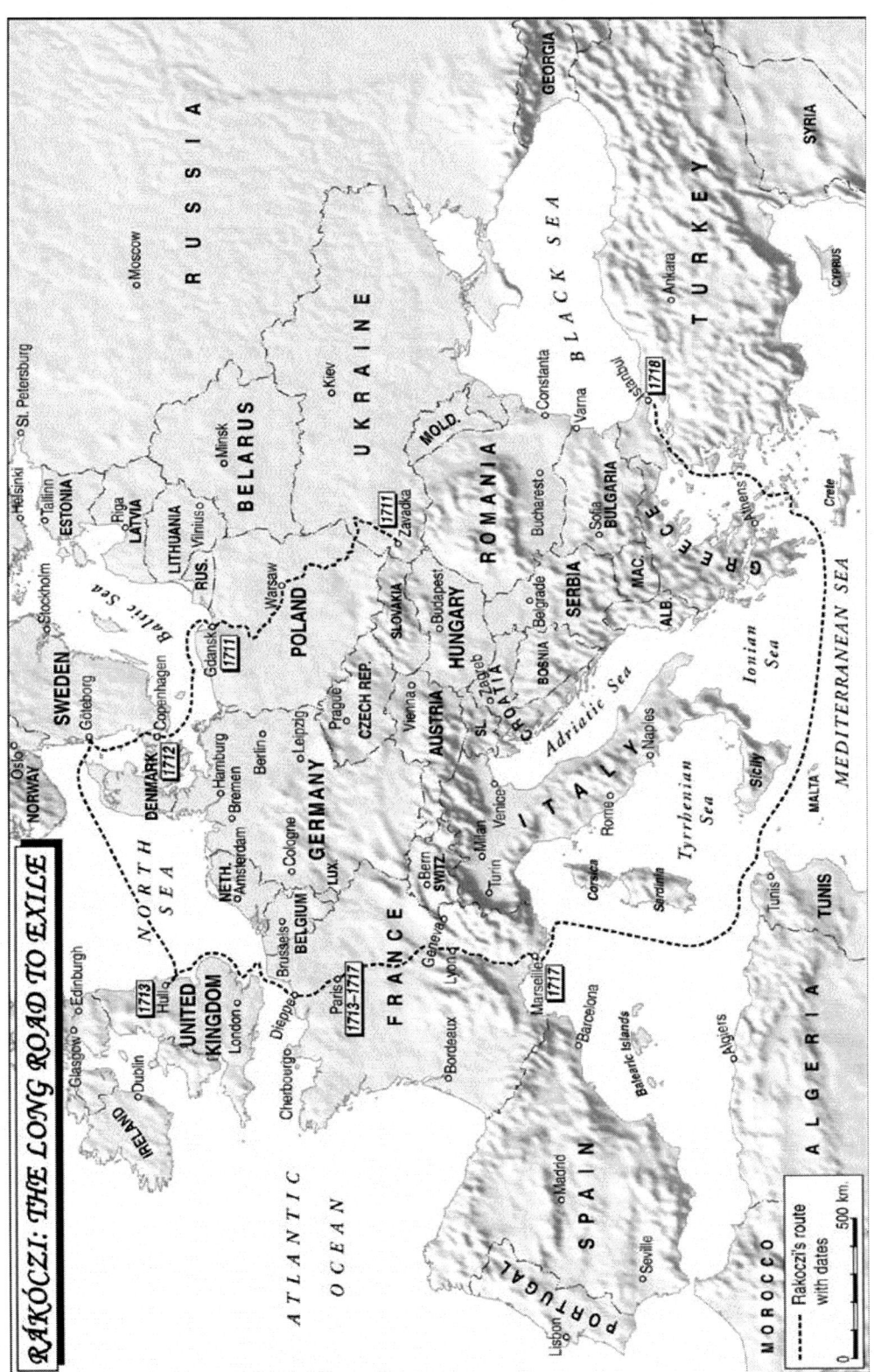

Chapter One
Prelude to Rebellion

The modern history of the Hungarians begins with the coronation of Stefan I as King of Hungary, on Christmas Day 1000 AD. With the blessing of Pope Sylvester II and the Holy Roman Emperor Otto III, this hallowed event marked Hungary's entry into Europe as a Christian state and, with the introduction of Latin as the official language, the beginning of its documented history. For a people who had arrived from the Steppes of Central Asia a mere 150 years before, it was a remarkable transition.

Despite constant bickering and feuding between Stefan's successors, the new Hungarian state prospered until the terrible year of 1241, when death and destruction were visited on Hungary by a murderous Mongol invasion: conservative estimates reckon that nearly half the population of two million perished either by the sword, pestilence or famine within 18 months. The Emperor Frederick II observed that the "entire precious kingdom was depopulated, devastated and turned into a barren wasteland". Recovery came slowly until the good governance of King Béla IV, when the country blossomed and went on to grow into a significant power under a succession of foreign kings—four Anjous from Naples, one Luxembourger, one Habsburg and three Polish Jagiellos. Then a new threat appeared from the East.

The Ottoman Turks, also known as "The Porte"[1] had been creeping West throughout the 14th century. By 1400, aside from the Dalmatian coast and a few cities in the Peloponnese, most of the Balkans were under the control of the Sultan; Serbia, Bosnia and Wallachia were vassal states—the once mighty Byzantine empire now consisted of Constantinople and a handful of small possessions.

Although allies during the Ottoman-Venetian war of the 1420s, Hungary and the Porte were destined to clash when Sultan Murad II reverted to the expansionist policy of his predecessors, setting his sights on all the lands

---

[1] Abbreviated from the French translation of the Persian *Bab-I Ali* or 'high doorway', a prominent feature of the Ottoman government building.

south of the Danube. His thwarted attack on the Hungarian fortress of Belgrade was more than offset when his successor, Mehmet II, captured Constantinople in May 1453, inflicting a devastating psychological blow on Christian Europe.

Two remarkable men held fast the Hungarian line, János Hunyadi and his son Mátyás. Having learned his military skills as a young condottiere in Italy, János raised a fighting force to face the Ottomans, leading a virtual one-man crusade: in 1442, he defeated Turkish attacks on Sibiu, the Iron Gates and the Ialomita River. Following the ringing of bells throughout Christendom on 29 June 1456 to 'plead with the heavens for a victory', three weeks later Hunyadi counter-attacked the Turks after they failed to maintain their siege on Belgrade. In savage hand-to-hand fighting, he decisively routed them. Such was the rejoicing at this victory, that even in far off Oxford in England, a solemn mass was held.

After Hunyadi's triumph at Belgrade, many believed the time had come to drive the Turks out of Europe, and perhaps even recapture Constantinople. But it was not to be. On August 11, 1456, Hunyadi died, most likely from the plague that had been ravaging Belgrade. Jubilation turned to sorrow when the world learned of his untimely death. Even Sultan Mehmet II paid him tribute: "Although he was my enemy I feel grief over his death, because the world has never seen such a man."

Although the Turks would not attack Hungary for another seventy years, political strife continued to haunt the kingdom. On his deathbed, Hunyadi exhorted his countrymen: "Defend, my friends, Christendom and Hungary from all enemies....Do not quarrel among yourselves. If you should waste your energies in altercations, you will seal your own fate as well as dig the grave of our country."

His son, Mátyás, was proclaimed King at the age of 15. He assembled a fearsome standing army that not only proved an effective deterrent to Ottoman territorial ambitions but also a formidable instrument of expansion. At one stage, in 1485, in addition to the Hungarian lands, Mátyás controlled Moravia, Silesia, Carinthia, Styria, Lower Austria and Vienna. On his death in 1490, his 'Black Army' was disbanded, leaving Hungary once again wracked by internal strife and hence exposed to the threat from the ever-avaricious Porte.

Prelude to Rebellion

A renewed Ottoman invasion of Hungary in 1521 began with the capitulation of Belgrade and then progressed to Mohács in the Danubian Plain, where five years later the Hungarian king, 21-year-old Lajos II, died in battle along with 16,000 of his men. His death was to have a momentous and lasting effect on Hungary. He had married Maria Habsburg in 1515, when they were respectively aged ten and nine, but died childless. However, his sister, Anna Jagiello, married Maria's brother Ferdinand, King of Bohemia, who now insisted on his rights to the Hungarian throne as set out in the succession contract the House of Habsburg had signed with the Jagiellos in 1515.

Marshalled by the widowed Queen Maria, the nobles of upper and western Hungary gathered at Bratislava on 17 December and elected the Habsburg Ferdinand as their king. However, the previous month, the Transylvanian and eastern Hungarian nobility had chosen János Zápolyai, the vajda or ruling warlord of Transylvania, as King and crowned him at Alba Julia. In the subsequent tussle for control, Zápolyai turned to the Porte, an act that would result in his ex-communication; it also brought into question the claim of Hungarians as defenders of the Christian frontier. The two kings finally came to an arrangement at Oradea in 1538, whereby the Habsburgs were awarded the right of succession in return for Zápolyai's son receiving financial compensation.

The former kingdom of Hungary was now split into three. To the east, Transylvania; in the centre and south, Ottoman-ruled Hungary and to the north and west, Royal Hungary, which in turn was divided into Upper Hungary—modern day Slovakia and south-west Ukraine—and western Hungary—modern day north-west Hungary and Croatia.

This Habsburg 'win' was a Pyrrhic victory since three years later the Turks captured Buda, the capital of Hungary, and soon after were firmly ensconced on the borders with Austria and the northern area of Hungary. Following the treaty of Edirne in 1547 when Hungary's division between the two powers was formalised, a military frontier[2] was established. By the late 1550s, a chain of more than a hundred fortresses, garrisoned by over 30,000 men, stretched from modern day Slovakia south to the Adriatic Sea.

---

[2] *Militärgrenze*, which was finally dismantled in 1878.

With the exception of small-scale incursions, this border defence system remained remarkably robust until the middle of the 17th century.

The Thirteen Years War of 1593–1606 between the Habsburgs and the Porte resulted in few gains for either side. The predominantly Protestant Hungarians were infuriated by the bloodthirsty actions of the Imperial General Basta in Transylvania, who had been charged by Vienna to enforce the Counter-Reformation as well as defeat the Ottomans. They saw him as a proxy for the militant Jesuits. Incensed by the Habsburg strategy to restore Catholicism to Košice in northern Hungary—95% of whose inhabitants were Protestants—in April 1605, at the Diet[3] of Szerencs, the Transylvanian Estates[4] elected a soldier, István Bocskai, as their Prince. His successful campaign in northern Hungary the following year, backed by the hajdus[5], resulted in the Treaties of Vienna and Zsitva-Torok in 1606, when Transylvania won its tentative independence.

Masterminded by the able Transylvanian diplomat, Gábor Bethlen, the outcome of the Treaties was indeed favourable to the Hungarians. Lutheran and Reformed churches were reinstated in royal Hungary; the prestigious office of Palatine[6] re-established with the appointment of István Illésházy; the finances of the kingdom separated from Vienna; all civil and military offices staffed exclusively by Hungarians; and the office of Prince of Transylvania confirmed in return for the incumbent conceding all claims to the Kingdom of Hungary. These agreements were to form the benchmark against which the Hungarians measured the good will of Vienna throughout the 17th and 18th centuries.

Most political thinkers of the day recognised that the reality of the new status quo meant that Hungarians had to live under three rulers—the

---

[3] A political assembly.

[4] The Estates comprised representatives from the (Hungarian) nobility, the Saxons and the Szekelys.

[5] Originally cattle drovers or landless peasants, hajdus/haiduks/ heyducks had served as irregular soldiers in the Imperial army before they defected and turned to banditry. The word came to mean brigand.

[6] When the Emperor was outside the boundaries of Hungary (which he usually was), the Palatine, elected by the Hungarian Diet, exercised the powers of viceroy

Prelude to Rebellion

Ottoman Sultan, the Habsburg Emperor and a Transylvanian Prince—and bide their time until the moment came to unite under their own elected King. The historian, László Kontner, sums up their dilemma: "Through the Habsburgs, royal Hungary could secure the indispensable external support to contain the Ottoman advance. At the same time, Transylvania could prevent—if necessary by relying on the assistance of the Porte— the Habsburgs from squeezing the nobility out of its positions in royal Hungary." Any deviation from this narrow path was to have grievous consequences.

During the next fifty years, until 1663, the military frontier between the Habsburgs and the Ottomans remained more or less unchanged. Ottoman territorial expansion to the West ceased: both the Sultan and his army focussed on a Mediterranean maritime strategy, including the attack on the Venetian-controlled island of Crete in 1645. However, the appointment of the Albanian, Mehmet Köprülü, to the office of Sadrazam (grand Vezir) in 1656 marked a turning point: the eleventh Sadrazam in a period of eight years, he was determined to bring the interminable Cretan war to a successful conclusion and to restore Ottoman supremacy in Hungary. To achieve this he had to rebuild the navy and restore discipline to an army which had become increasingly soft and mired in politics, nepotism and corruption, as well as reaffirm control of the provinces which had become far too independent. His solution was simple: over the next five years, 35,000 'offenders' were executed on his orders.

During this time, the Hungarians did not endear themselves to the Habsburgs: Gábor Bethlen and György Rákóczi I, Princes of an independent Transylvania, had both joined the Thirty Years War on the side of the Bohemians and Moravians against the Habsburgs. Both had emerged with creditable peace treaties (Nikolsburg in 1621 and Linz in 1645). The message to Vienna was clear: the Hungarians were unreliable, and soon mercenaries recruited from abroad were sent to replace Hungarian castle captains and border fortress soldiers.

On 27 June 1655, two weeks after his fifteenth birthday, Leopold Habsburg was 'elected' and crowned King of Hungary. He was one of a triumvirate of rulers who all succeeded to their thrones around the same time; his cousin, Louis XIV to the French throne in 1661 and Mehmet IV to the Ottoman Sultanate in 1656. These three men were to dictate events in Hungary and Transylvania during the next half-century.

Destined by his father to be Bishop of Passau, Leopold had been exclusively educated for a career in the Church until his elder brother's sudden death from smallpox. His teacher, the Jesuit Neidhard, became Grand Inquisitor on return to his native Spain. Leopold's Jesuit education had such a profound effect on him that some contemporaries believed he was worthy of canonization.

Protestant commentators held a less flattering view: "Leopold was fitter for the confessor's box than for the throne. In him the Jesuits had a king after their own heart. … His appearance was as unkingly as it is possible to imagine. Diminutive in stature, his lower jaw protruding horribly, his little bald head enveloped in an immense peruke, surmounted by a hat shaded with a black feather, his person wrapped in a Spanish cloak, his feet thrust into red shoes, and his thin tottering legs encased in stockings of the same colour as if he had been walking up to the knees in blood, he looked more like one of those uncouth figures which are seen in booths than the living head of the Holy Roman Empire." This version by James Nisbet of his ungainly appearance is supported by the Venetian ambassador, who somewhat more diplomatically described him as 'favoured by fortune, if not by nature'.

Leopold's principal advisers—the Grand Chamberlain Prince Portia, the President of the Aulic War Council[7] Prince Lobkowitz and the commander-in-chief General Montecuccoli—confronted by a renewed Ottoman threat, wanted to place Hungary firmly under the control of Imperial troops, an idea that was not initially favoured by the Hungarians.

In his book, *Hungary in the Year 1677*, Montecuccoli wrote that the Hungarians were "proud, restless, voluble, impossible to satisfy. They retain the nature of the Scythians and the Tartars, from whom they originate. They yearn for unbridled licence….a Proteus every one of them, now loving and now falling out of love, quick to raise up and quick to bring low, they demand at one moment and reject the next." He strongly believed that the only way to govern the Emperor's Hungarian subjects was to force them to conform to Vienna's will; in a word, they needed to be 'Germanized'.

---

[7] Hofkriegsrat created in 1556 to manage military operations.

Prelude to Rebellion

In the late 1650s, Russia was also confronted by the Ottoman menace, unable to access the Black Sea and its lucrative Mediterranean markets. To the North, its gateway to the rich trade with the Baltic States and England was blocked by Charles X of Sweden. When Jan II Kazimierz of Poland refused to recognise Charles's accession to the Swedish throne in 1655 and formed an offensive alliance of Austria, Russia, the Netherlands and Denmark, Charles sounded out the Prince of Transylvania, György Rákóczi II, and proposed that Rákóczi should claim the Polish throne for his own dynasty.

For Rákóczi, this was too good an opportunity to miss. If he could secure his election as Polish King, then with the help of the Voivodes of Moldavia and Wallachia whose support he had enlisted in 1653 and 1655, together with his own Transylvanian resources, he would be able to expel the Turks from Hungary. By June 1657 he had occupied Warsaw, but a Danish attack diverted the Swedes and the combination of Russian, Polish and Austrian troops under Montecucculi forced him to sue for peace at the immense cost over one million forints and he scurried back to Transylvania, leaving the bulk of his 20,000 army as prisoners of the Tatar Khan. Destined for the Crimean slave markets, most never returned home.

That autumn, Rákóczi was given the chance to redeem himself on the international stage when a group of Hungarian noblemen—including Nikolai Zrinyi, Ban of Croatia, Ferenc Wesselényi, Palatine of Hungary, Ferenc Nádasdy, Lord Chief Justice of Hungary and György Lippay, Archbishop of Esztergom—all promised him armed assistance if Transylvania would hold firm against the Turks. For their part, the group would ask Leopold to do likewise in return for which they would lobby for his election as Holy Roman Emperor at the forthcoming College due to assemble that August in Frankfurt. The French and Swedish embassies were known to be busily scheming against him. Vienna responded to this overture with a vague promise of a few thousand troops.

While the wily Sadrazam Köprülü had no reason to support Poland—before his death, Leopold's father Ferdinand III managed to conclude a treaty with Russia for the defence of Poland—he had every reason to bring Rákóczi to heel for he knew that the Prince had been conspiring with the rulers of Wallachia and Moldavia, both vassal states of the Porte, to undermine Ottoman suzerainty. On the grounds that Rákóczi's invasion of Poland exceeded his authority as an Ottoman appointee, Köprülü ordered his removal and the Transylvanian Estates compliantly elected a more malleable Prince in the person of Ferenc Rhédey. Stung by this craven subservience to the Porte, Rákóczi wasted no time and immediately deposed him.

Soon after his successful election as Holy Roman Emperor in 1658, Leopold notified the Porte that he did not intend to break the peace on behalf of György Rákóczi or anyone else, thus triggering a major Turkish invasion of Transylvania; the capital Alba Julia capitulated, the countryside was laid waste, much of the population sold into slavery and towns forced to pay exorbitant funds to stave off further attacks. The Sadrazam then nominated Acatius Barczai as Prince of Transylvania, raised the annual tribute from 15,000 to 50,000 florins and demanded reparations. Yet again, it had all gone disastrously wrong for the ambitious György Rákóczi and Transylvania. More ominously, Leopold had sown the seeds of distrust which were to be reaped in a bloody harvest of disaffected Hungarians throughout his long reign.

The stalwart Rákóczi refused to give in and appealed to Leopold for help. The Emperor was hardly in a position to send assistance—he had not forgotten Rákóczi's invasion of Poland and, more to the point, he had no standing army. Even though his most able lieutenant, János Kemény, had returned from captivity in the Crimea, and with help from the new rulers of Wallachia and Moldavia, Rákóczi was in a political cul-de-sac, up against the might of the Porte while the Habsburg Holy Roman Emperor sat it out on the sidelines. Although the Voivodes of Wallachia and Moldavia initially resisted Ottoman attacks, by the end of the year the unstoppable Ottoman military machine prevailed, forcing both rulers to flee into exile. With no allies left, Rákóczi continued the fight alone and was mortally wounded by Ottoman soldiers at the battle of Gilău in May 1660. As his body made its last journey to his ancestral home at Sárospatak, the Turkish commander launched a ferocious attack on the remaining defenders—both men and women—of the castle at Oradea. Such was the magnitude of their heroism, that when the siege finally ended in August, as a gesture of respect the Ottomans allowed them to depart with all their possessions.

Prelude to Rebellion

In January 1661 János Kemény was chosen by the Estates as Prince of Transylvania and the hapless Barczai executed. Supported by the Palatine and the chief nobles of Hungary, Kemény again appealed to Leopold for help when the Porte's Tartar mercenaries began ravaging the Székelysfold and Paşa Ali of Timişoara attacked the Saxons in the Siebenbürgen[8]. The Emperor's usual response to such a crisis was "to pray rather than to scheme", but on this occasion he had to act fast and despatched Montecucculi with a force of 10,000 men to assist the Prince. The Turks saw this as overt recognition of Kemény and quickly arranged for the Transylvanian Estates to elect an Ottoman nominee, the meek and timid Mihály Apafi. A former prisoner of the Tartars and a man of great learning, Apafi was to prove time and again during the next thirty years that he was not the soft touch his Ottoman masters had initially thought.

Montecucculi linked up with Kemény in Upper Hungary and together they marched to Cluj. The Turks refused to give battle, a tactic which exasperated the great Field Marshal. On 15 September, leaving 2,000 men behind, Montecucculi told Kemény he was retiring to the Tisza valley for the winter. In fact, he was obeying new orders from Vienna: Mehmet Köprülü, busy in Crete trying to retake Candia from the Venetians, had offered Leopold a deal. If he recognised Oradea as an Ottoman possession and withdrew his assistance to Kemény, the Porte would abandon its punitive raid against Transylvania. Unbeknown to Kemény, Leopold had accepted this offer and although Kemény nearly succeeded in capturing Apafi at Sighisoara that winter, he was killed by a Turkish relief force on 23 January 1662. Never had the hand of the Porte rested heavier on Transylvania.

Mehmet Köprülü had died in November 1661; his son Ahmet Köprülü, duly appointed by the Sultan to succeed his father as Sadrazam, temporarily ceased hostilities with the Habsburgs. Now it was the Hungarians who demanded the withdrawal of German troops from their territory, those very same troops Rákóczi and Kemény had implored the Emperor to send them in previous years.

Vienna, appalled by the ingratitude of the Hungarians, opened negotiations with he Porte at Timişoara and put its military plans on hold: with funds

---

[8] In central and southern Transylvania.

scarce, any diplomatic straw was worth clutching if potential cost-savings came with it. The Turks had a different agenda and, with no intention of reaching an agreement, in the late spring of 1663 the Sultan and Köprülü led an army of 120,000 men to Belgrade, the Sultan only reaching as far as Edirne where he decided to spend the summer hunting. Realising that any defence of Transylvania was impossible against such odds, the Estates fell in behind their Ottoman-sponsored Prince, Mihály Apafi.

Fed with accurate intelligence by his ambassador at the Porte, Leopold sensed that time was running out and summoned the Imperial Diet to Regensburg in January 1663. It took the rest of the year for the electors to reach agreement to send a force of 20,000 (under the command of Prince Louis of Baden Baden) to counter the Ottoman threat.

When Köprülü reached Budapest in late summer, all that remained between him and Vienna was Montecucculi with 6,000 men and a string of forts along the Danube. One of these, Nové Zámky, held out till 25 September, thereby delaying the Turkish advance until the next year. While the Ban of Croatia Nikolai Zrinyi conducted a brilliant campaign deep behind Ottoman lines, the dire news of a Turkish army heading west even triggered a response from France; Louis XIV sent the Comte de Coligny and 4,000 men to join Montecucculi.

On 1 August 1664, as Köprülü's army attempted to enter the Austrian province of Styria, despite a military superiority of three-to-one, it was defeated by Montecucculi at the battle of St Gotthard on the banks of the Raab River. Under attack from two directions, the Turkish infantry broke ranks and fled towards the river, where many drowned, preventing Köprülü from crossing with the remainder of his forces. Montecucculi had comprehensively outmanoeuvred his far larger opponent, helped by the young and impetuous Duke Charles of Lorraine (future brother-in-law of the Emperor), who drove his cavalry regiment through the enemy's left wing, capturing the Turkish flag as a trophy. However, his depleted and exhausted army failed to counterattack and exploit this unexpected success for Vienna was preoccupied with impending events in the west.

Louis XIV was preparing to seize his 'inheritance' from the ailing and childless Charles II of Spain, the last of the Spanish Habsburgs. But Bavaria and Austria also had valid claims to the Spanish territories, which included Spain, southern Italy, Sardinia and the Spanish Netherlands. With the balance of power in Europe at stake, the last thing Leopold wanted was an extended campaign in the east. His financial and military resources were running dry. This was the predicament that would dog him throughout his reign and was reflected in the division of his court into 'Easterners' and 'Westerners', or 'the Spanish faction': there was only enough money to prosecute a war on one front and even then, funds were usually insufficient.

Relations between Leopold and Louis were to dominate the affairs of Europe for the next forty years. As Professor Spielman writes in *Leopold of Austria*: "Louis saw Leopold as a pompous young incompetent who stood in the way of his glory; Leopold regarded Louis as an insufferably arrogant hypocrite whose deceitfulness was matched only by his bumptious disregard for the convention of good behaviour. Both men misjudged the other and often acted impetuously from a deep and shared mistrust."

On balance, Leopold had more to fear that Louis. France had a population of eighteen million, against Russia's fourteen million, Austria's six and a half million, Spain's six million and England's five and a half million. Paris with half a million citizens was Europe's largest capital. But behind these statistics, poverty was endemic, financial disorder widespread and the legal process corrupt. Massive reductions had been made in the French army in 1662 to pay for tax cuts to alleviate the plight of the peasantry.

After their defeat at St Gotthard, the Turks were pleasantly surprised to be offered exceptionally generous terms. At the Peace of Vasvár on 10 August 1664, it was agreed that both the Emperor and the Sultan were to withdraw their troops from Transylvania; Prince Mihály Apafi was to remain "master unmolested" and the Estates would elect a successor in the event of his death; the Turks could keep their gains at Oradea and Nové Zámky and retain suzerainty[9] over Transylvania but they had to demolish their fort at Sered; the Emperor could build a new fort on the Váh River at Leopoldov; a 20-year 'term' was to be applied to the treaty, after which it could be renewed; finally the Emperor contracted to pay the Sultan 200,000 florins a year. These terms were drawn up by Prince Portia the leader of

---

[9] A sovereign state having supremacy over another state which has its own ruler but cannot act independently.

the Westerners and were so secret that not even Apafi or senior officers of the Imperial army knew of their existence until the Proclamation of 7 September, two months after the Treaty had been signed.

From Leopold's perspective, these terms were acceptable since he faced an unpredictable situation in the West, unrest in Hungary and Transylvania and an economic crisis. To the Hungarians, however, the Treaty of Vasvár made no sense at all. How could such advantageous terms have been negotiated by the Turks when they had been soundly beaten on the battlefield? Why had the Emperor and Montecuccoli failed to follow up their victory and drive the Turks out of Hungary? As the rebel leader Count Imre Thököly put it in *His Memoirs*, "The Hungarians saw themselves thereby abandoned to the Turks". The immediate impact was the continuing presence of Imperial troops who had been billeted in north-west Transylvania since 1660; they were socially undesirable and a financial menace, more accustomed to looting country houses than restricting themselves to the tedium of garrison duties.

The dissatisfaction with Vienna's policy expressed by the Hungarian higher nobility fell on deaf ears. Leopold and his ministers had noted that with the exception of Nikolai Zrinyi they had scarcely played any part in Montecuccoli's campaign and were noticeably absent at the decisive battle of St Gotthard. Reports reached Vienna from France that Louis XIV would almost certainly invade the Spanish Netherlands and probably the Franche-Comté as soon as Philip IV died. This is exactly what happened: 18 months after Philip's death in September 1665, Louis' troops crossed the frontier.

Religious friction also aggravated the heavy financial burden of funding the Imperial garrisons. As Count Imre Thököly later recalled:

"The Protestants in the mean time were so ill treated in the places where the Catholics were the strongest that several of them would rather venture to fall under the Protection or Dominion of the Turks, who does not force the Transylvanians to take up the turban, than be exposed to the caprices of a Prince absolutely governed by the Jesuits, a more barbarous sort of people, said the Hungarians, than the Dervices."

After living with the dismemberment of their nation for the last 120 years in the shadow of Vienna and the Porte, the dejected Hungarians yearned for the reunification of their lands and the return to political independence. The events of 1664 were to prove a dramatic turning point.

Chapter Two
The Magnates' Conspiracy

The reaction to the Peace of Vasvár by the magnates[1] of Hungary and Croatia[2] veered from disbelief to anger. All their hopes for independence had been dashed. Before long the idea to mount a moral and legal challenge to the Habsburgs gained ground: either honour the terms of the 1606 Peace of Vienna, including the prized *ius resistendi* (which allowed the nobility to take up arms against the King in the event of disagreement) and religious freedom for all, or face rebellion. It became known as 'The Magnates' Conspiracy' by the Habsburgs and the Uprising by the Hungarians.

This was no run-of-the-mill plot by a few nationalist hot-heads from the hinterlands of Upper Hungary and Transylvania: the ringleaders were none other than Leopold's top officials in Royal Hungary, of which first and foremost was Nikolai Zrinyi, the Ban of Croatia, the outstanding poet, soldier and thinker of his generation. The Zrinyis were one of the most illustrious and well-connected of all the families in Royal Hungary. At the end of the 12th century, the Subic family from Bribir, after inheriting the title of Prince, commensurately increased their power, and by the outset of the 14th century Pavao Subic governed Bosnia as far as the Drina River. Later on they acquired the town of Zrin, hence the name Zrinyi, and in the 16th century, they took control of Medjimurje (the county in the northernmost part of Croatia.) with its capital at Cakovec. Enormously wealthy, the family owned more than 200 villages, extensive forests and mines and several trading ports on the Adriatic.

The first Zrinyi to rise to international fame was Count Nikolai. As a 21-year-old soldier, he distinguished himself at the siege of Vienna in September 1529, and in 1542 saved the Imperial army from almost certain defeat at the gates of Budapest by intervening in a well-judged sally with

---

[1] Hereditary lords of a province, the highest ranks of the nobility.
[2] An integral part of the Hungarian Kingdom since the 'Contract of Union' at the beginning of 12th century.

his small band of 400 Croats. In token of his appreciation, the Emperor appointed him Ban of Croatia (King's deputy).

In August 1566, Nikolai once more confronted the Turks. For five weeks and with a garrison of only 1,000 men, he held up Sultan Suleiman the Magnificent and his 30,000-strong Turkish army at the fortress of Szigetvár to the west of Pécs. In a desperate last stand, Zrinyi ordered the gates to be thrown open. His men fired two heavy cannons point blank into the enemy ranks. Then, at the head of his 300 remaining soldiers, Zrinyi stormed out of the fortress. He was fatally wounded and only three of his men survived. In a last act of defiance, the women and wounded blew themselves up in the ammunition tower, taking many of the attacking Turks with them. All told, the Battle of Szigetvár claimed the lives of 2,500 Hungarians and Croatians and 25,000 Turks. During the siege, the Emperor Maximilian, waiting nearby with a large army, chose to ignore Zrinyi's calls for help-it was the height of the duck shooting season and he did not want to interrupt his sport. For his gallant action, Zrinyi won the posthumous epithet of "Hero of Szigetvár" and a place in the history books.

His great grandson, Nikolai, also started his career as a soldier on the military frontier. Well-educated and fluent in six languages, the intellectual Nikolai owed his choice of a military career to the simple fact that "the buried bones and ghosts of Hungarian heroes won't let me sleep." The difference between them was that his great grandfather had been party to a central formalized defensive organization separating warring factions, but by the early 17th century the Ottomans and Habsburgs wanted peace on the frontier. As a consequence, both reduced the number of soldiers serving in their border fortresses, allowing the landowners and Paşas to become increasingly influential. In the case of Hungary, this empowered the Batthyánys, Zrinyi and Nádasdy families to become 'Lords of the Border'.

Thus, aged seventeen, as a Captain General, Zrinyi took over command of the Croatian border fortress zone. With 5,000 men, he faced around 10,000 soldiers of the Ottoman Paşalik at Nagykanizsa. It was here he honed his military skills on weekly raids, snatching prisoners and rustling cattle. On one such escapade, he managed to steal the Paşa's horses. Nikolai was soon dubbed 'the master of the small war'.

The Habsburgs

A youthful Leopold

Leopold in old age

Joseph I

Charles VI

The Ottomans

Kara Mustafa

Mehmet IV

Ahmet Köprülü

Ahmet III

The Conspirators (I)

Petar Zrinyi

Nádasdy

Nikolai Zrinyi

Wesselényi

The Conspirators (II)

Lippay

F.K. Frangepán

The executions at Wiener Neustadt

Helena and Imre

Helena the heroine

Helena the bride

Thököly in his prime

Thököly in exile

Ferenc Rákóczi II

Boy

Young man

Amalie

Prince of Transylvania

Rákóczi's generals

Károlyi

Ráday

Bottyan

Beresényi

The Habsburg generals

Heister

Rabutin

Caraffa

Montecucculi

The Magnates' Conspiracy

In 1645 he fought the Swedes in Moravia, scattering a division at Szkalec and taking 2,000 prisoners. A general at the age of 26, he saved the Emperor at the fortress of Eger, which had been surprised by the Swedish mercenary general, Wrangel. He went on to rout the army of György Rákóczi II on the Upper Tisza, for which he was appointed Captain of Croatia by the Emperor. In 1652–53, he was fighting the Turks but found the time to marry the wealthy Eusebia Draskovics and to write a number of military treatises including *A Small Tract on Military Encampment and A Valiant Lieutenant* (though they were never published in his lifetime). At the coronation of Ferdinand IV, Zrinyi carried the sword of state and the Emperor made him the Ban and District Captain General of Croatia in 1649.

The relationship between Zrinyi and Vienna was forthright if not always positive. In November 1650, he went to Vienna to complain about Habsburg interference with the lucrative cattle trade to Venice. If the Aulic War Council wanted to maintain the border defences against the Turks, these trading revenues were essential to the local economy: the rapacious Austrian treasury grudgingly relented. The following year, Zrinyi intercepted a message from the Sadrazam to the Paşa of Nagykanizsa, which confirmed his analysis that Turkish military supremacy was rapidly coming to an end. The Sadrazam advised the Paşa to exercise vigilance since the overall strategic outlook was bleak—the Poles had beaten off the Tartars and were threatening the Crimea, the Venetians had destroyed the Turkish fleet that July and the Persians were limbering up in the East. After passing the message to Vienna, word came back to Zrinyi that there was to be no concerted action against the Porte.

Sensing the danger of an impending Ottoman invasion, Zrinyi wrote a passionate position paper—*"Turkish Poison: Don't harm the Hungarians! Medication Against Turkish Poison"*—in which he called on his countrymen to face the impending threat:

> "Since God burdened me with the love of my country, I hereby shout and scream: Hear me, Hungarians who are alive. Here comes the peril. Here is the consuming fire! And what is there to be done? Weapons, weapons, weapons are desired, and a good valiant resolution".

In Vienna, the assessment of the Turkish threat once more differed from Zrinyi's. After the death of Prince György Rákóczi II in June 1660, the court believed that the danger of war with the Turks had subsided. Hence all hostilities were to cease and Zrinyi was ordered to abandon his siege of Nagykanizsa. The absurdity of this policy became evident when the Turks seized Oradea and then proceeded to rampage through Transylvania. A thoroughly alarmed Aulic War Council promptly despatched Montecucculi to go to the aid of Prince Kemény and at the same time put Zrinyi on full alert. He immediately placed an order for ten canons to be cast in Vienna. His plan was simple and straightforward: to evict Turkish forces from Nagykanizsa and roll up the southern flank of the Ottomans, eastwards along the Drava River.

In 1661, Zrinyi began to frustrate Turkish attempts to reinforce Nagykanizsa and embarked on an ambitious project to build a fort on the banks of the Mura River five miles to the south of the town. He sent a memo to Vienna that July, outlining his plans. However, he was not prepared for what happened next. The Sultan had the Paşa of Nagykanizsa executed for incompetence and at the same time sent a barrage of diplomatic notes to Vienna complaining about Zrinyi. The result was an order to halt further construction at the fort.

The situation was far from satisfactory. While the Ottomans regrouped and reorganised their defences, Montecucculi's troops maltreated the Protestant population in Upper Hungary, who in desperation turned to Zrinyi to act as their spokesman. It was a measure of the esteem he was held in, for Zrinyi was a Catholic. At the Diet in Bratislava, he made his displeasure clear on the matter of the ill discipline of Montecucculi's men, a spat which led to open mutual dislike between the two generals.

By 1663, the talk in Vienna was about the Spanish succession and the threat posed to Habsburg interests by Louis XIV. It was almost as if the Ottomans were no longer present. Zrinyi hastened to Austria in May and managed to persuade the Aulic War Council to send 6,000 troops to defend the border in Styria. Concurrently, he continued with the construction of his new fortress on the Mura and raised a force of 20,000 to defend it. By July, as a Turkish army of 100,000 set off from Belgrade towards Vienna, Zrinyi was authorised to attack Ottoman positions in his area of operations.

Granted the title of Commander-in-Chief of all Hungary, he set about his new orders with enthusiasm. In November he was abruptly relieved of his title, no doubt due to the meddling of Montecucculi, and the army was split into three separate commands—Souches in the north, Montecucculi along the Danube and Zrinyi on the Drava River.

In 1664, Zrinyi set out from Cakovec to destroy the Turkish-held bridgehead at Osijek on the Drava River in order to cut off the Turkish army's line of retreat. After a brilliant winter campaign lasting 26 days, during which his forces covered over 450 kilometres, he succeeded in his mission but was unable to exploit the advantage due to the reluctance of the other Imperial generals. In consolation, the Emperor offered him the title Prince with the congratulation: "I envision a resurrection of the Christian name in the wake of your wise and brave enterprises." The Pope struck a commemorative medal and wrote: "The Ottoman Empire seems to be seized by fear, while the Christian peoples of the Earth are seized by hope and spirit caused by the strength of one man." The Spanish King sent him the Order of the Golden Fleece and, much to his surprise, Louis XIV gave him 10,000 gold ducats.

In response, the Turks surrounded the Zrinyi family home at Uj-Zerin. While Zrinyi hastened to relieve it, Montecucculi did nothing, which triggered a vitriolic war of words between the two generals, resulting in Zrinyi conducting a lively pamphlet campaign:

> "You received a wonderful army and destroyed it without fighting the enemy, you molested your friends more than your enemies; you looked on passively while the Turks carried away over 100,000 Hungarians. Such behaviour is worse than that of a villainous hangman".

In return, Montecucculi accused Zrinyi of being "a military illiterate."

Given the strength of his feelings, it came as no surprise when Zrinyi resigned after the Peace of Vasvár. Though he tempered his resignation with a promise that he would assist the Emperor at any time with a force of 6,000, his patriotism had led him to the conclusion that Hungary's decline under the Habsburgs was fast becoming irreversible. What was needed was an independent Hungary, united under a national ruler, whose first task would be to drive out the Ottomans. Before this could happen, a strong and efficient Hungarian national army had to be created. There was only one candidate for the job of raising and leading it—Nikolai Zrinyi.

Zrinyi contacted his fellow magnates, Nádasdy, Lippay and Wesselényi, to form a secret council. His motive was simple: Leopold was clearly acting against the interests of Hungary. He should be deselected as King and a new candidate elected by the Estates, one who would pledge to free the country from Ottoman rule as well as honour the *ius resistendi*. At this stage there was no religious agenda for the ringleaders were nearly all Catholics. The French soon heard of their grievances and in a letter discovered many years later, Louis XIV wrote: "I was in secret contact with the Count Zrinyi in order to stir up trouble in Hungary in case I started a war against the Emperor."

A week before the Hungarian leadership was due to meet the Emperor in Vienna, on 18 November 1664, aged 44, Zrinyi was killed on his estate at Cakovec by a wild boar. The family motto, *Sors bona, nihil aliud* (Good fortune; nothing else) on this occasion let him down. Or was it murder? One source states that a Habsburg soldier in his retinue shot him. Another source named Ferenc Nádasdy, since they were in fierce competition for high office. However there were two eye witness accounts to the fatal incident. Young Miklós Bethlen, who was staying with him at the time, records a huntsman telling Zrinyi that he had wounded a boar. Zrinyi jumped on a horse and rode off in pursuit of the wounded animal. Miklós and his companions followed and found Zrinyi dead, face down on the ground: "there were three wounds to his head; one on the left above the ear, where the boar's tusk had penetrated to the bone, tearing the skin of his head towards the forehead; a second was also on the left, on his cheek below the ear….the third was on the nape of the neck towards the throat, and had severed all the tendons in the neck;…. it is a mystery why so brave a man neither fired nor struck at the boar, having to hand both Stutz (a pistol) and sword." Zrinyi's sister-in-law, Ana Katarina, was staying at the castle. In her diary, discovered years later in a convent in Austria, she wrote: "When they brought him in, he bled to death. If there had been a surgeon to stop the bleeding, he would probably have survived."

The Hungarians revere Zrinyi as "a warrior poet":

> 'As long as time endures, my name shall sound
> in distant Scythia, whence the Magyars came,
> in all lands where their exploits still resound,
> to men who know their honour and their fame.
> I have earned fame not only with my song
> But also with this warrior's sword men dread—
> I battled with the Turk my whole life long,
> And joyed to strew my homeland with their dead'[3]

There was also another, more tender side to his poetry. Here he writes about the death of his first son in the spring of 1659:

> "My lovely little bird, my little nightingale, ah! Suddenly indeed has he flown away; in him was all my hope, but he rose and departed from me like a thin shadow."

Nikolai Zrinyi's legacy to Hungary was the intellectual template on which all future rebellions against the Habsburgs were based. The overriding imperative was the need for allies abroad; Hungary could never shake off Habsburg rule in isolation. Yet, at the same time, it had to rely on its own military resources. As Zrinyi put it, "foreign help was never a substitute for self-help."

Petar Zrinyi inherited the title of Ban on the death of his brother. A year apart in age, both had been educated by the Jesuits in Graz and travelled together to Italy but that was where the similarities stopped. In 1639, they had split their family holdings, with Nikolai remaining in Cakovec and Peter setting up court in Osalj, a hundred miles away. This was unusual and suggested an incompatibility between the two brothers. Professor Kalsan of Cakovec Castle explains: "In temperament, Nikolai was brave but modest, with interests in art and scholarship. He was a competent soldier, an able administrator, thoughtful strategist and bold tactician. In contrast, Petar was explosive, acting unconsciously by rushing into things without thinking. And their wives also acted in very different ways: Nikolai's—first, Eusebia Drašković, then Barunica Sofia Löbl—were always in the background, but

---

[3] From Zrinyi's The Epilogue.

not so Petar's Ana Katarina, who was a very strong personality and often signed official papers on her husband's behalf. When it came to raising international support for the uprising, it was Katarina who was sent to Venice by her husband."

Despite maintaining good relations with Vienna, when command of the family fortress at Carlovac was given to the Imperial General Herberstein as Captain General, it became clear to Petar that the *realpolitik* behind Austrian post-Vasvár policy was one of occupation. Zrinyi moved to strengthen his position and recruited his bother- in-law, Fran Krsto ("F.K.") Frangepán, a poet and the translator of Molière's *Georges Dandin* into Croatian. More out of frustration than conviction, Zrinyi also contacted his much disliked first cousin, Ferenc Nádasdy III, in Bratislava and a friend, Count Erasmus von Tattenbach in Graz, using F.K. as a go-between.

While hardly a threat to Vienna, F.K.'s family name was revered in Croatia. The Frangepáns were first mentioned in 1133 as the rulers and lords of the island of Krk. They rose to prominence in the 14th century when Prince Ivan V became Ban of Croatia and Dalmatia, a post the family held more or less uninterrupted until 1622. Through political astuteness and marriage, they amassed huge estates in what is today's Croatia and Slovenia.

In Upper Hungary, the conspiracy gathered momentum under the leadership of the Palatine, Ferenc Wesselényi, with the blessing of the Cardinal György Lippay, Primate of Hungary and Archbishop of Esztergom, who recently had had his family estates confiscated by Vienna. After the death of his first wife Žofia Bosniak at Strečno in April 1644, Ferenc found himself in charge of the Imperial troops with orders to besiege the Castle of Muráň which had raised the colours of György Rákóczi II over its battlements. To Wesselényi's amazement, the castle was defended by a 34-year-old woman, the beautiful Maria Széchy, granddaughter of the notorious Countess 'Dracula' Erzebert Báthory and Ferenc Nádasdy. Estranged from her second husband, Maria had moved in with her sister, to whom the castle belonged. Struck by the absurdity of two Hungarians at war with each other, Wesselényi arranged a truce and entered the castle to negotiate with "the Venus of Muráň". The outcome of their talks came as a surprise: the antagonists buried their differences and married that July.

Wesselényi's neighbour, the bucolic Count István Thököly, quickly pledged his name to the conspiracy. The Thökölys lived in the remote castle of Arva, high up in the foothills of the Tatra Mountains. They had made their fortune out of dealing in wine and cattle, with a few advantageous marriages en route. Count István was depressed by the financial ramifications of the Treaty of Vasvár, which threatened to destroy his livelihood. His lucrative trade in driving Hungarian cattle up the Danube through Vienna to Germany had been ceded to the Austrian-controlled Oriental Trading Company. When the young Miklós Bethlen went to stay at Thököly's castle at Kežmarok in 1666, he found "dreadful entertainment, drinking, dancing, music, hunting and other pastimes, filled more than a week, because István Thököly outstripped all the lords in Hungary, and the other Estates too, indeed, in that wickedness…the master of the house and the other guests around us were drunk every wretched day, and quite often twice in a day."

Wesselényi was now anxious to include the wealthy and influential Rákóczi family in his inner circle. Prince György Rákóczi II had been killed fighting the Ottomans at Oradea in 1660, leaving a 16-year-old son, Ferenc Rákóczi I as his heir. With their stronghold at Mukachevo and estates at Sárospatak and Tokay, the family had become—along with the Eszterházys—the richest and most exalted in Hungary; they could travel a hundred miles without leaving their lands. Wesselényi came up with a proposition. He suggested marriage between Petar Zrinyi's beautiful, well-educated and high-spirited daughter, Helena, and Ferenc I. Rákóczi's mother, Zsófia, concurred for Helena "had beauty, a penetrating wit and a way to insinuating, that it was capable of gaining the most rebellious of hearts". After their wedding at the Castle of Zborov (today in north-east Slovakia), in 1666 the young couple moved to Sárospatak, one of Rákóczi's many stately homes.

The last Hungarian magnate to be recruited to the inner circle, and by all accounts the most reluctant, was Ferenc Nádasdy III, the Lord Chief Justice of Hungary. The Nádasdy family, one of the oldest in Hungary, included some of the most distinguished courtiers and soldiers of the day. Tamás, born in 1498, had been chosen to offer the Hungarian crown to Archduke Ferdinand of Austria. Through a judicious marriage and with endowments from the new King, he went on to amass enormous land holdings. Made

Ban of Croatia, then Commander-in-Chief, he became Count Palatine in 1554. His son, Ferenc Nádasdy II, known as the Black Prince or 'Fekete Beg' by the Turks, excelled as a soldier, recapturing from the Ottomans four crucial fortresses, a feat of arms recognised by Vienna with rewards of yet more land and money. His son Pál became Commander-in-Chief but died aged 36, leaving Ferenc Nádasdy III to continue the family tradition of soldier, statesman and benefactor of education and the arts. He was elected Lord Chief Justice at the same time Wesselényi became Palatine.

Nádasdy joined the magnates at their third meeting. Although virulently anti-Protestant—he had 'ruined' around 200 Protestant parishes in Western Hungary—he was prepared to bury his religious differences with his fellow conspirators and present a united front in their opposition to the House of Habsburg.

The only non-Hungarian member of the conspiracy was the Styrian Count Hans von Tattenbach of Graz, who was the commander of the southern border fortresses. A nineteenth century account states that Tattenbach had indeed been loyal to the Emperor until March 1670, but the Austrian secret services had decided to compromise him. The instrument of their chicanery was two scoundrels, including a former chaplain of the Tattenbach's, who induced him to use 'imprudent language' and then denounced him. Another version states that Tattenbach was married to the Hungarian Countess Forgách and had been enticed into the conspiracy by the promise of land. Professor Spielman describes him as a lover of Katarina Zrinyi.

Here were the highest nobles[4] in Royal Hungary, Croatia and Styria—Zrinyis, Frangepáns, Wesselényis, Lippays, Thökölys, Rákoczis, Nádasdys and von Tattenbachs—lined up against their Emperor, more in anger than ambition, frustrated by Habsburg callousness, despairing of Leopold's despotism and deeply resentful of the political and economic repercussions of the Counter Reformation. It was no use conspiring among themselves. Real help in finance and arms lay abroad and so the question in 1665, as they gathered at the remote Wesselényi castle of Murán high up in the Nízke Tatry hills, was: Who to turn to for help?

---

[4] The lesser nobility were represented by a loquacious and excitable lawyer, István Vitnyédy.

The Magnates' Conspiracy

There were several options. Poland's geographical proximity to the north of Royal Hungary made it the ideal ally. However, King Jan II Kazimierz, still indebted to the Emperor for his help against Charles X of Sweden, was now engaged in a long struggle with Russia in the Ukraine. But with French influence on the ascendancy in Warsaw—Kazimierz's queen, Louise Marie de Gonzague, proposed the French Duc d'Enghien as the successor to her husband and the Commander-in-Chief of the Polish army, Jan Sobiewski, married to a Frenchwoman, Marie d'Arquien, was also favoured by Paris—an alliance with Poland seemed likely. Then, despite the manoeuvrings of the French, the Polish Diet elected as king a Pole, Michael Wisniowiecki, in June 1669. The following year he married Leopold I's sister, Eleanora Maria, and thus the door closed on Poland as the magnates' ally.

In the summer of 1666, Mihály Apafi, the Prince of Transylvania, was sounded out by the conspirators. He despatched Mihály Teleki and Miklós Bethlen to Muráň, where they agreed that the Tisza River would constitute the border between Hungary and the independent Principality of Transylvania, if and when the Turks were evicted. But Transylvania had neither the money, the men nor the influence to put any rebellion on a sound footing.

Their next ploy was to put together an anti-Habsburg alliance with Venice and France. The Venetians were not interested since they were over-extended in the Mediterranean. France, an ally of the Ottomans since the days of Francis I, was a different story: Louis XIV saw an excellent opportunity to cause trouble for the Holy Roman Emperor without having too much involvement. His envoy in Vienna, Comte Grémonville, met with Nádasdy and Zrinyi in a village inn outside the city walls, all heavily disguised. Letters were set to Versailles and Constantinople, and envoys despatched to Edirne and Warsaw. Another envoy was despatched to the Sadrazam who was campaigning at Candia in Crete. Soon the Magnates' Conspiracy became the worst kept secret in Europe, a daily topic of conversation in the courts of Venice, Vienna, Warsaw and Constantinople.

When Ferenc Wesselényi unexpectedly died at Muráň on 27 March 1667, Nádasdy was nominated by the Hungarian Diet to replace him as Palatine. Leopold, in his capacity as King of Hungary, over-ruled this decision and appointed Cardinal Szelepcsényi in his place. Nádasdy pointed out to the

Emperor that this act was illegal and drew his attention to the growing dissatisfaction among the Hungarian nobility. The warning was lost on Leopold.

On his part, Petar Zrinyi now considered the formation of an independent principality in Croatia and Slavonia. He approached Omer-Spahia, the Sultan's son-in-law and commander of the Ottoman army in Bosnia, with a set of proposals: any territory conquered in an offensive against Vienna belonged to Croatia if Croatian and to Hungary if Hungarian; Croatia's liberty would be respected by constitutional decree, and Croatia would pay a tribute to the Sultan as long as he guaranteed that liberty. These overtures were scuppered either by Sadrazam Köprülü himself or compromised by an Austrian spy. News of this plot reached Vienna on 12 June, although the Porte did not reveal the names of the conspirators.

In 1668, a whispering campaign started against Nádasdy in Vienna. Among the more preposterous accusations circulated by the Emperor's agents were that he had set fire to the Emperor's apartment in Vienna, he had offered the Emperor a poisoned pastry and he had poisoned the Emperor's water supply by dropping a dead dog into it. Leopold was well-informed by Grand Chamberlain Lobkowitz about the antics of the conspirators but it seemed that they hardly constituted a serious threat. Hungarians were notorious for their dislike of Habsburg authority, or for that matter any authority. It was equally clear that by 1668 the French would not underwrite a general uprising in Hungary but merely continue to dabble in Magyar nationalism.

Ferenc Rákóczi I now summoned the remaining conspirators, together with a new recruit, Ferenc Bónis, to his castle at Sárospatak. In a room on the first floor, seated under a rose motif painted on the vaulted ceiling, he reminded them that as a child he had been chosen by the Transylvanian Estates to succeed his father as Prince of Transylvania. Then he recalled how he and his mother had re-embraced the Catholic faith in 1661 when they returned to Sárospatak after the death of his father at Oradea. This in turn made him the de facto temporal leader of the Catholics of Upper Hungary. If his fellow conspirators would support him in his claim to the Principality of Transylvania and urge the Estates to elect him, in return he would acknowledge the primacy of the Hungarian Reform (Protestant) church in any future independent state of Hungary, thereby guaranteeing the compliance of the Catholic population. This was the crux of the Sárospatak Declaration signed in 1669.

Rumours about the conspiracy continued to circulate. Take the case of this account of Leopold's illness in April 1670:

"Indescribably gloomy was the chamber of the royal patient: the candles looked as if they burned in a tomb; the atmosphere was mephitic; the king's face wore the ghastliness of the grave; his sallow skin and sunken cheeks, with the thirst which nothing could assuage, gave indubitable signs that some unknown poison was at work upon him. The celebrated Milanese alchemist, the Chevalier Francis Barri, paused and looked round the room. "You are breathing a poisoned air," he said to the king. The patient's apartment was changed, other candles were brought, and from that hour the king began to recover. Within a month, Leopold was cured."

When the candles were analyzed it was found that the unused tapers contained over two and a half pounds of arsenic. A dog, which was given a piece of the wick to eat in its food, died within three hours. It is hard to imagine what motive the Jesuits, who were in charge of Leopold's quarters, could have had for his murder, and there is no evidence that this botched assassination attempt was the work of the Hungarians. The finger might point at Louis XIV, since Leopold had no heir at the time to inherit the possessions of the Spanish Habsburgs. The affair still remains a mystery. As for Barri, one would think the man who saved the king's life would have been rewarded. Instead, he was handed over to the Papal envoy, who claimed him as his prisoner and threw him into the dungeons of St. Angelo in Rome, where he died fifteen years later.

After five years of such rumours, Leopold and Prince Lobkowitz were finally forced to act to forestall an imminent insurrection. When they heard that Protestant preachers in Upper Hungary were giving thanks to God for the Turkish victory over the Venetians in Crete and calling on the Porte to "rescue Hungary from oppression and Papist slavery" and that Ferenc Rákóczi I had summoned the leaders of the Protestant counties to Košice, the Emperor and his advisers reacted quickly. The Estates of Upper Hungary were ordered to assemble at Banska-Bystrika on 16 March 1670. They refused and sporadic fighting broke out. The Privy Conference met in Vienna the following week, and troops were ordered to quash the insurrection. Austrian soldiers entered Croatia and Silesian cavalry moved into Upper Hungary. Austrian, Bohemian and Moravian units took control of the Váh valley. Lobkowitz posted a price on the heads of Zrinyi and Frangepán and confiscated their estates. The office of Ban of Croatia was transferred to the loyal Count Miklós Erdödy.

Events moved fast. On 22 March, Count Tattenbach, betrayed by a servant against whom he had instigated criminal proceedings for theft, was arrested and copies of the correspondence between the conspirators seized at his home. The same day General Herberstein commenced operations in Hungary. Within a month, both Zrinyi and Frangepán set off for Vienna on the understanding that they were protected by Lobkowitz's offer of Imperial clemency. As far as Zrinyi was concerned, the agreed terms included that he was not to be treated as a rebel—his life, liberty, estates and honour were to be respected in return for which he would hand over his son to Vienna as a hostage and resign as Ban of Croatia. Ominously, the day after Zrinyi and F.K. left, Imperial forces arrested Zrinyi's wife Katarina. When the two men reached Vienna, they were immediately arrested.

On 1 May, the northern rebels led by Rákóczi and Bocskai threw in their hand after twelve days of fighting. By August, the Imperial Generals Spork and Duke Charles of Lorraine had recaptured all the fortresses taken by the rebels. One such fortress was Muráň which yielded an unexpected bonus; Wesselényi's widow, Maria, was betrayed by her secretary and all her late husband's correspondence with the conspirators seized. She was given no choice other than to accompany the incriminating correspondence to Vienna.

Initially, Leopold was inclined to follow a relatively benign course of action, in the hope that he could win back the trust and loyalty of the magnates. Both Lobkowitz and Archbishop Szelepcsényi, the Palatine, were in agreement with him. After all, Hungary had been disarmed, its chief nobles incarcerated and all meaningful resistance suppressed. However, the evidence was so damning that legal proceedings were started and a show trial set in motion. The preliminary investigation by the Imperial Chancellor Hocher and the Secretary of the Privy Conference, Christof Abele, unearthed evidence of a plot to murder Leopold; such a serious allegation had to be sent to a special court of twelve High Court functionaries (none of whom were Hungarian). In early April 1671, Zrinyi, Nádasdy and Frangepán were found guilty of "an innumerable company of crimes and wickednesses" and sentenced to death. Still hoping to avoid their execution, Leopold presented the verdict to a commission of privy councillors and High Court officials. They found in favour of the death sentences, as did the Privy Conference, which met in Leopold's presence on 25 April.

The verdict on Petar Zrinyi read: "He committed the greatest sins than the others in aspiring to obtain the same station as his majesty, that is, to be an independent Croatian ruler and therefore he indeed to be crowned not with a crown but a bloody sword".

His final letter to his wife, Anna Katarina, suggests a man who was never cut out to be a rebel leader: "My dear Soul! I most humbly beg of you, that you would not grieve your self to excess, at the sight of this letter. Tomorrow, Ah madam, I must tell it you, Alas! Tomorrow about ten of the clock in the morning, we must lose our heads, I, and your brother. To day we have taken our last farewell each of other; and now I come also to take leave of you, my Dear Soul, for ever; entreating you that you will please to pardon me all things, whereby in all my life time, I have ever offended you. God be thanked, I am very well prepared for death, and fear nothing; having a sure hope that God who hath created me, will have pity on me, whom I shall also beseech, for I hope I shall tomorrow be in his presence, that we may see each other in eternal glory before his throne…. God preserve and bless you' and my daughter Aurora Veronica, Amen".

F.K. was distraught; he begged for a stay of execution, protesting he was too young to die and furthermore he was the last of his line. He wrote a last minute appeal to Leopold:

"Dread Sovereign, I am scarcely able to hold my pen for the great consternation wherewith I am seized by reason of the cruel and unexpected sentence which against me miserable wretch hath been pronounced this afternoon: my strength and courage fail me, O Emperor Most Gracious! To write to you, as my necessity requires, so as to excite in your Imperial Breast one small spark of mercy for the saving my life…Neustadt, 28 April about 11 o'clock at night."

The spark of mercy never materialised for Leopold could not have overruled his Privy Council. Furthermore, he felt that due process of law had been exemplarily carried out. F.K. then penned a letter to his wife:

F.K. then penned a letter to his wife:

"My dear Julia, I wish from the bottom of my heart that I could leave you some pledge of my faithful love. But alas! I find I am poor and bereft of all things....Farewell, my dear Julia, farewell; farewell my entirely beloved companion; as we have in this world lived in Peace and Love, so in the other world I shall be your most faithful advocate before his Divine Majesty. My dear Julia, I ever remain your most affectionate and most faithful husband."

Both Zrinyi and F.K. asked that the sentence of having their right hands cut off be commuted since they believed it would hamper their chance of salvation. The authorities promised to look into it. As they were separated, ready for the scaffold, F.K. turned to Zrinyi and said: "I hope that tomorrow we shall embrace and kiss each other with greater joy and contentment than we have now done here below." It was the last time they were to see each other. F.K. perhaps would prefer to be judged as a poet rather than a politician: "Right now come together to the glorious flag.

> Dispel from your heart all vapours of fury;
> Put before you the shield of courage;
> Dearer to you will be glory, fame and honour,
> Than one instant, one moment of living, in shame:
> He who dies honourably lives forever".

This last line served to inspire Hungarian patriots for centuries to come.

On 30 April 1671, at 10 a.m., Nádasdy was executed in the market square in the centre of Vienna, an event watched by Hagi Ibrahim, the Turkish Chiaus, who reported to the Porte that Nádasdy had met justice. Other members of the nobility had been summoned to watch. After the event, they were forced to inspect the body. One witness wrote: "They saw the prince laid in a coffin, dressed in Hungarian attire, with his head on his chest, almost floating in the blood that half-filled the bier." The next morning, Zrinyi and Frangepán were executed in the square at Wiener Neustadt. It was a clumsy performance by the executioner: two blows of the axe fell before Zrinyi was cleanly decapitated. As for poor F.K., the first blow struck his right shoulder, and as he tried to raise himself from the ground, the second severed his head. At least they had been allowed to keep their right hands. On 1 December 1671, Count von Tattenbach was executed at Graz; three blows of the axe were needed to remove his head.

Vienna now pursued the Zrinyi family. Petar's son, Ivan Antun, was imprisoned in the mountain fortress of Kufstein, where he was held without trial for the next 30 years. He eventually went mad and died in 1704, aged 50. His mother, Ana Katarina, banished to a Dominican convent in Graz, also lost her mind and died in 1673. Her two daughters, Judita Petronela and Aurora Veronika were both confined to convents in Zagreb and Klagenfurt respectively, where they died aged 47 and 75. The Zrinyi estates at Cakovec, having first been pillaged by General von Spanckau, were confiscated.

However, for the last surviving male Zrinyi, Adam, it was a story of Imperial clemency. Only two when his father Nikolai was killed, Adam was brought up in Vienna, where he became a great favourite of Leopold, who made him a Brigadier General in 1683. The following year, Leopold attended his wedding to Maria Lamsburg. It was Adam who passed on the news of the Ottoman capitulation at Buda to Leopold in 1686. Promoted to Field Marshal the following year, Adam officiated as Marshal of the Kingdom of Hungary at the coronation of Joseph I as King of Hungary. Killed at the battle of Slankamen in 1691, aged 29, Adam's body was buried in Vienna.

The families of the other conspirators fared little better than the Zrinyis. F.K's son died at an early age. All Wesselényi's property was confiscated, his widow imprisoned and the Emperor's captain destroyed the family's fortress at Strečno. In 1670, Count István Thököly was besieged at his castle at Likava and killed by Imperial troops: his body was left to rot in the cellars for nine months. His son and heir, the 13-year-old Imre, was smuggled out of the castle dressed as a poor villager and then, disguised as a young Polish girl, was spirited through the Austrian lines to safety in Transylvania. His three sisters were sent to Vienna, where they were converted to Catholicism.

Nádasdy's properties were confiscated and sold. His children, stripped of the right to use the Nádasdy name, were compelled to call themselves Von Kreutz (from the village where the Nádasdy printing presses were installed) and the males made to wear red silk cords around their necks, imitating the mark made by the axe on their father. The family shunned politics for many years while Ferenc Nádasdy IV worked diligently to rehabilitate the family's name and repossess its estates, four of which were returned in 1713 by Emperor Charles VI. Ironically, Ferenc Nádasdy V married Maria Rottal, the granddaughter of Count Johann Rottal, who had been instrumental in his grandfather's prosecution, and went on to distinguish himself as an Imperial soldier. It was largely thanks to Nádasdy's Hungarian hussars that the Empress Maria-Theresa's army won a major victory against the Prussian forces at the battle of Kolin in Bohemia in 1757.

The cycle of rehabilitation from Hungarian rebel to Imperial court favourite had taken 86 years.

The Emperor Leopold, a volatile mix of Christian piety and political ruthlessness, ordered 2,000 Masses to be said for the souls of the departed nobles. This pious instruction was qualified: the Masses were to be paid for out of the proceeds of the confiscated estates.

One conspirator, Ferenc Rákóczi I, conspicuously avoided the executioner's axe. Following the intervention of his mother Countess Zsófia and her Jesuit contacts, Ferenc escaped with his life by paying a massive fine of 400,000 thalers, reduced from an initial demand for two million thalers. Despite his enormous wealth, Rákóczi had to borrow 100,000 from his mother, 20,000 from the Primate and 47,000 from the Jesuits. Forced to leave his castle at Sárospatak, he died at the family's manor house at Borša on 8 July 1676 leaving his glamorous and feisty widow, Helena Zrinyi, daughter Juliana, and three-month-old son Ferenc II. After his death, Helena was allowed to move to the remote Castle of Regéc, where there was more room to bring up her young family.

As a result of the suppression of the Magnates' Conspiracy, Leopold was considerably richer. In addition to Rákóczi's fine and the income from the sequestered estates, Nádasdy's castle had yielded over 4 million forints in cash. As for Louis XIV, that master of "blowing the horn to excite the pack", he dropped a note to his cousin Leopold, congratulating him on the "detection of this dangerous conspiracy".

The military occupation now underway in Royal Hungary merely served to incite Hungarian nationalism. Imperial troops pillaged, raped and committed acts of sacrilege against Catholic and Protestant churches alike. The soldiers, infrequently paid, made up for their lost wages by looting Hungarian towns and villages. Furthermore, Leopold decided that the Hungarians should pay for the upkeep of the Imperial troops stationed in Hungary. On 21 March 1671 he issued a decree which made every county responsible for the upkeep of each soldier on its territory. By June, after widespread protests, the amount had been halved but the levy still rankled.

Two special commissions were formed in Bratislava to follow up charges of involvement in the Magnates' Conspiracy by other members of the Hungarian nobility: one chaired by the Austrian Count Rottal and the other by the Hungarian chancellor Miklós Pálffy. As a result, by the end of 1671 more than 2,000 people, many of them Protestants, had been imprisoned on suspicion of rebellion and an extraordinary court established to deal with the cases. If found guilty of treason or rebellion, the nobility forfeited their estates to Vienna; the old Hungarian rules of passing them to a member of the family no longer applied. Three Counts, István Thököly, István Vitnyédy and István Csáky were tried posthumously and found guilty.

The Privy Conference now began to examine a series of proposals designed to strengthen Habsburg control over Hungary. Suggestions ranged from the abolition of the elective nature of the Hungarian monarchy to the elimination of Protestantism throughout the country. Even the continued existence of the Diet and the counties were called into question. Leopold was deeply unhappy about these ideas since they were in direct conflict with his coronation oath. The counter-argument was that it was the magnates themselves who had contravened their oath and hence Leopold was not bound to his. Still, he remained undecided and it was only in February 1673 that he finally sanctioned the creation of a new office of governor, with a seven member governing body based at Bratislava and directly appointed by Vienna.

The first governor, Count Ampringen, Grand Master of the Teutonic Knights, soon realised that his new office merely served to rally anti-Habsburg sentiment and warned Vienna against any further suppression of the Hungarians. But politics had been overtaken by religion: it was Archbishop Szelepcsényi's co-ordinated campaign in 1672 to close down the Protestant schools that triggered riots in the towns of Upper Hungary. That summer Leopold decreed that all Protestant preachers should leave Hungary. Joined by the equally fervent Catholic Bishop Kollonics, Archbishop Szelepcsényi assembled a special court at Bratislava in January 1674. The results were quick and spectacular: 26 Protestant ministers were marched off to the galleys of Naples, 733 Protestant intellectuals exiled or imprisoned and under the personal direction of Kollonics, around 800 Lutheran churches were 'recovered' by the Catholics. Hamel Bruynincx, the Dutch ambassador to Vienna, circulated an account of these events, causing profound unease throughout Protestant Europe.

The major error made by Ampringen's court was that it confiscated estates belonging to nobles who had not even taken part in the revolt, a sure recipe for insurrection. Undoubtedly a number of Catholic nobles exploited this anti-Protestantism in order to enrich themselves with the confiscated estates of their own countrymen. The Habsburg-controlled Orientalische Compagnie was awarded exclusive buying rights in the occupied territories, thus forcing the flourishing Hungarian cattle trade into bankruptcy, just as the late Count István Thököly had feared. It was indeed ironic that one of the largest customers of the Orientalische Compagnie was the Ottoman Paşa in Turkish-occupied Hungary. Another error was the decision to disband over two thirds of the Hungarian garrisons of the border fortresses. This merely served to create a pool of unemployed soldiers, ideal recruits for a guerrilla army.

The methods advocated by the martially-minded Montecucculi and Leopold's Jesuit advisers, who thought that the Hungarians could be broken by terror, were deeply flawed. Here is a typical piece of advice from Montecucculi to Leopold: "It is not possible to keep these ungrateful, unbending and rebellious people within bounds by reasoning with them, nor can they be ruled over by tolerance or ruled by law. One must fear a nation that knows no fear. That is why its will must be broken with a rod of iron and the people sternly kept in their place….After all, the ferocity of a restive steed cannot be controlled by a silken thread, but only with an iron snaffle." As Professor Richard Lodge observed, a 'Bohemian' solution to the Hungarian problem was inappropriate for "the Magyar, though inferior as a plotter, is, however, a more resolute rebel than the Slav."

The response to this heavy-handed Habsburg strategy was predictable and dangerous: from August 1672 the *bujdosok* (from bujdoso meaning 'hiding'), small groups of political refugees and displaced persons, went underground or crossed into Transylvania and started a guerrilla war in Upper Hungary against the Imperial army. Prince Apafi of Transylvania acted as their patron and his right hand man, Count Mihály Teleki, became their de facto commander. International support from France followed, for the very existence of the *bujdosok* gave the lie to Leopold's claim that he had pacified Hungary. Within weeks, General Kopp arrived from Austria to deal with these first signs of insurrection. He defeated the *bujdosok* at Györke near Presov on 26 October 1672, thereby relieving General Spankau who had been besieged at Košice. The *bujdosok* were characterised by a deep hatred for Austria and a loathing of Catholic Hungarians. Often based across the border in Transylvania, where their activities were tolerated by the Turks, the *bujdosok* mounted raids into Upper Hungary where they attacked small Imperial garrisons with spectacular cruelty, torturing and mutilating their victims and taking no prisoners. This in turn provoked an equally brutal response from the Imperial forces, turning the guerrilla war into a savage tit for tat conflict. The *bujdosok* raids continued into the summer as Leopold had to withdraw nearly all his troops to fight France in the West.

The death of the Polish King Wisniowiecki in November 1673, while the country was still at war with the Ottomans, resulted in the election of Jan Sobiewski as the new King on 21 May 1674. Bound to France by his wife, Marie, and her political associates, it was not unexpected when he signed the Declaration of Warsaw with Louis XIV in June 1675. Poland was to receive a subsidy and French military assistance in restoring its sovereignty over East Prussia. In return, Louis was allowed to recruit Polish soldiers for his army and Poland was to lend a helping hand to the Hungarian rebels or 'mécontens' as the French termed them. In the years ahead, Louis paid out one million livres tournois to the Hungarians rebels. The first result of this alliance was the advance of the French Colonel Comte Boham at the head of 3,000 Polish volunteers to the very gates of Vienna. With coins inscribed "Ludovicus XIV, Galliae Rex, Defensor Hungariae", these soldiers of France caused the diversion of 30,000 Imperial troops from Germany to Hungary. It was an excellent first investment.

Early encounters between the French-led *bujdosok* and the Imperial unleashed a savagery that was to characterise the war. In 1675, Imperial troops captured a French officer, the Comte de Dampierre. He refused to talk under interrogation and when left unguarded in his cell, he bit through his veins and bled to death. The following year, the Comte de Boham, after winning a skirmish against General Schmidt, confronted General Kopp outside Košice. Kopp's Hungarian soldiers promptly deserted him, leaving him no option but to retreat behind the city walls. Enraged, he proceeded to execute six members of the Hungarian nobility who were his prisoners of war: two were roasted alive and the others impaled. From then on, woes betide any Imperial soldier captured by the *bujdosok*. Soon, excesses were perpetrated by both sides. Leopold recalled Kopp and replace him with Count von Würben, who had strict orders to spare his prisoners' lives.

Meanwhile, Poland was still at war with the Turks in the Ukraine: despite his victory over them at Lemburg in 1675, Sobiewski was forced to the conference table and in October 1676 signed the treaty of Zuravno—the Turks kept most of Podolia but recognised Polish suzerainty over Western Ukraine. The Sadrazam Ahmet Köprülü died shortly after; his successor Kara Mustafa conveyed to the French court his intention to attack Austria without delay. Then the situation changed. The Cossack Hetman, angered by the treaty of Zuravno—after all, the Cossacks had originally appealed to the Porte for help against the Poles—now turned to Russia. From 1677 to 1681, the Cossacks and their new allies, the Russians, engaged in a conflict with the Turks that absorbed both Ottoman time and resources.

Following their successful alliance with the Poles, the French nominated the young diplomat Francois Bethune to meet with the Transylvanian envoy, Daniel Absolon, in Warsaw in May 1677. Together they hammered out an alliance whereby the French agreed to fund the Hungarian exiles in Transylvania and support any large-scale military action against Leopold. In return, Transylvania would provide the exiles with a general, Mihály Teleki, and other military commanders and guarantee a retreat area where they could rest undisturbed. The French further undertook to defend Transylvania against any punitive expedition by the Ottomans and to represent Transylvania's interests at any future peace conference.

Leopold meanwhile played the marriage card again. This time he offered his daughter's hand to Sobiewski's son. The offer was accepted and Sobiewski publicly reneged on his pledge to aid the *bujdosok*.

For the Hungarians, the Magnates' Conspiracy began and ended in shambles. It had never been conceived as a premeditated war of independence, for its origins lay in frustration and anger over the sudden Habsburg capitulation to the Ottomans at the Treaty of Vasvár. Hamstrung by lack of leadership after the untimely death of Nikolai Zrinyi, the only man capable of orchestrating a serious revolt, the conspirators stumbled along the road to perdition, their security compromised and their planning non-existent.

The historian R.W.Evans finds elements of political farce: "The existence of a privileged caste both made the plotting possible and also ensured its failure. Pampered but not courted, that caste was able to nurse rebellion while possessing neither the heart for a serious breakaway nor any understanding of political realities. Precisely because of the covert bond of high Counter-Reformation culture, Nádasdy could expect clemency from Leopold (whom he had regularly and regally entertained at his castles); precisely for want of any overt political bond between Vienna and Hungary it could not be granted: indeed, all manner of improbable rumours were circulated about the dissidents' plans and readily believed in Austria and abroad. Thus the same evidence was bound to be interpreted in two different ways, and the death sentences proved just as surprising to the magnates as they were obvious to most of the rest of Europe."

As they mounted the scaffold, the principal perpetrators of the plot conducted themselves with dignity; ignominy fell on the Habsburgs as the Imperial executioner clumsily tried and failed to behead his charges in one clean blow. There was a hidden warning here for Leopold: the Hungarian people were not going to give up easily, for tenacity, courage and obstinacy were deeply engrained in their national character. Suppression, in the short term, may have offered a workable strategy but it was never going to provide a lasting political solution.

Chapter Three
Imre Thököly and Helena Zrinya

The canny Mihály Apafi, Prince of Transylvania, had begun to distance himself from the insurrection; his enthusiasm to confront the Imperial oppressor had started to wane when immediate results were unforthcoming. In 1678 his military representative, Mihály Teleki, relinquished command of the rebel forces and suggested a successor—the dashing young Imre Thököly, who happened to be engaged to his beautiful widowed daughter. During the dramatic siege of the castle of Likava in 1670, the 13-year-old Imre had been smuggled out by two noblemen and given refuge with the Teleki family. Dispossessed by Vienna of his family's estates, incensed by the aggressive activities of the Jesuits and deeply patriotic, the young Thököly was the perfect choice to lead the rebellion.

From the beginning, Thököly proved himself to be a charismatic leader, with an intuitive understanding of the need for showmanship in order to rally the disparate ranks of rebels. Here is a description from his *Memoirs* of one of his meetings with the Turks: "One hundred and fifty Hussars well-mounted, with Trumpets and Kettle-Drums. One of them carried a standard of a blue colour, where one might see in Gold an Arm with a Naked Sword in the hand and the name of Thököly about it. There was also a red standard with his Arms and some others with six lead horses. Five hundred Hungarian gentlemen followed. Then came Thököly himself. There were six persons with tiger-skins upon their backs, clothed in the Hungarian fashion, with a grey cloak lined with white wolves' skin, with edges of silver upon the hems and long white feathers in their Caps. There followed a coach and two calashes, with a Green Standard at the Head of a Company of Heyducks well appointed and armed. At last came a troop of cavaliers."

His tactics were 'hit and run', emerging out of the morning mist and disappearing into the evening gloom. He favoured open country where his horsemen excelled; he avoided fortified towns since he lacked siege engineers and logistical support. In 1678, looking for supplies, Thököly reached Mukachevo, the stronghold of the Rákóczi family in north-east

Hungary. While attempting to introduce himself to Rákóczi's widow, Helena (née Zrinyi), he suddenly found himself on the receiving end of an attack organised by her mother-in-law, the formidable Zsófia Báthory—it was Zsófia who had saved her son Ferenc Rákóczi I from the executioner's axe through her Jesuit connections. As far as she was concerned, Thököly was a Lutheran, a rebel and a 'gold digger' after Helena's fortune: on all counts, he was an undesirable suitor and an unsuitable step-father for Juliana and Ferenc. His troops retired in disorder.

According to a French version of his courtship of Helena, Thököly, disguised as a peddler, found his way into the Castle, and having opened his pack and shown her several trinkets, presented Helena with her portrait in miniature, encased in a gold box, set with diamonds of great value'.

For the rebels, international support was now ebbing away. Earlier that year, Leopold had called the magnates and prelates to assemble in Bratislava to discuss an end to the insurrection. Encouraged by what they saw as a retreat from the Imperial reform programme and a relaxation of the fiscal regime, the magnates instructed their chancellor, Pálffy, to demand the withdrawal of all Austrian troops from Hungary. The Imperial Chancellor, Hocher, sensing bad faith, persuaded Leopold to withdraw the mooted concessions, and thus the rebellion resumed that summer.

In October 1678, Thököly attacked Kremnica and other mining towns in Upper Hungary and made off with an enormous booty of coin and unminted silver, estimated at 180,000 ducats. His lieutenant, Colonel Joshua, a former monk who had forsaken his robes and turned Protestant, entered Austria with troops gathered from impoverished Hungarian families but contented himself with pillaging rather than a purposeful military campaign. By the end of that year, little had been achieved. With their strongholds in Upper Hungary retaken by Imperial troops, Thököly, Imre Pálffy and their French adviser, Colonel Boham, were holed up at Debrecen on the border with Transylvania; Pál Wesselényi, the son of the former leader of the Magnates' Conspiracy, found quarters at Baia Mare. The rebels had much to think about for nothing of any political or military significance had been achieved so far.

Leopold, still trying to find a way to a lasting settlement with the rebels, tentatively opened negotiations with Thököly at Sopron that winter. The

Archbishop of Grán listened to Thököly's demands: a complete and full pardon, the restoration of the Hungarian constitution and reinstatement of the office of Palatine, the restitution of Protestant churches, the banishment of certain Catholic priests and sufficient security arrangement to ensure his requests were fulfilled. His response was to demand that Thököly lay down his arms as a precondition of any talks. Thököly refused.

The following spring, Thököly and Wesselényi fell out, unable to agree on a common plan. It was a plague year as well, which brought most military movement to a halt. On the international stage, the Peace of Nijmegen with France relieved Leopold's forces in the west. With no immediate threat from Turkey or Poland to support the rebels, the Emperor was in a position to turn his full attention to the problem of how to deal with the Hungarians. He had come to the conclusion that the way to a lasting accommodation was not through persecution but conciliation. As Claudio Magris writes in *Danube*, 'the Habsburg art of government does not stifle dissidence or overcome contradictions, but covers and composes them in an ever-provisional equilibrium, allowing them substantially to go on as they are and, if anything, playing them off against one another. The ruler allows his citizens to pass from love to rebellion and vice versa, from depression to euphoria, in a game without end and without progress'.

By 1679, Thököly and Helena were passionately and publicly in love. For Helena, it was also a chance to get even with the Habsburgs who had beheaded her father, imprisoned her brother without trial, banished her two sisters to convent life and presided over the death of her grief-stricken mother. Her property on both sides of her family had been confiscated and given to the Imperial Chancellery. Even as Rákóczi's widow, save for her household expenses, all the revenues from his great estates went to Leopold since young Ferenc was his ward. However, before any marriage to Imre could take place, there remained the formidable impediments of the Countess Zsófia and the Emperor.

That year the zealous Count Ampringen was recalled to Vienna and the following year, 1680, a truce arranged with Thököly, who asked the Emperor for permission to marry the beautiful Helena. If allowed, he offered to convert to Catholicism and support the Emperor, providing his estates were returned. His request was refused.

Now the *bujdosok* became *kurucs* or rebels (from the Turkish word *kurudsch* for rebel); Thököly recaptured his estates at Lipto and Arva, and then took the key town of Košice. Helena was overjoyed: "If Fortune has lately crowned you, it is love must settle your throne. You have subjects, but you have not any towns where you can keep your court. You may come to Mukachevo when you will, and settle there the seat of your empire. You shall reign, wherever I am Sovereign. For you have been so long the Master of my Heart, it is but just you should be so of my Dominions."

In February 1681, Leopold, still in a conciliatory mood and alert to rumours of impending war with the Porte, summoned a Diet at Sopron. He was prepared to give ground: Article One of the Peace of Vienna was to be maintained; religious freedom given to Hungarian soldiers; the office of *gubernium* abolished and that of the Palatine reinstated; the Hungarian Treasury to revert to its former independent status; a complete amnesty for all, including Thököly, and the construction of Protestant churches permitted in a large number of towns. In effect, Leopold renounced for ever the hope of unifying the Habsburg Empire through the imposition of Roman Catholicism. Professor Berenger sums it up: "The result was that the only possible unifying bond between all the peoples of the House of Austria did not, and never did, exist. The patent of tolerance of 1681 was only a realistic admission of failure intended to avoid even worse ills."

Despite Leopold's appointment of the pro-Hungarian Prince Pál Eszterházy as Palatine, Thököly refused to attend the Diet. Instead he sent three envoys to demand that Protestants should have rights to worship freely and to own property. The problem with this demand was that if Leopold accepted it, he would have to restore to the original owners all the Protestant property confiscated or sold to date. Faced with a tricky decision, Leopold dithered and did what he was best at: he waited for events to force his hand. News soon reached him that the French had seized the Imperial city of Strasbourg. Convinced that another war with France was imminent, he restored the Peace of 1606 in Hungary, affording complete religious freedoms in the towns. However, he still ducked the property issue and the confiscated Protestant estates remained in Imperial and Catholic hands.

Thököly now turned to the Porte, offering the Sultan suzerainty over Hungary. This was not constructive, as Professor Lodge explains: "From the

Austrian point of view, he acted as the hireling of France and as an ambitious and unscrupulous rebel who was at all costs resolved to gain a principality for himself. From the opposite point of view, he was the resolute defender of political and religious liberty who refused to be deluded by the deceptive promises of an intolerant despot—promises which were only extorted by fear of France and Turkey and would be withdrawn as soon as that fear had disappeared."

In September 1681 Thököly set out to attack the Imperial troops in Upper Hungary, synchronising his operations with the continuing French encirclement of Strasbourg in the West. A mixed force of 17,000 Transylvanians, Wallachians, Moldavians and Turks, all under the command of Mihály Apafi I, Prince of Transylvania, and his military adviser, Mihály Teleki, linked up at Debrecen with 8,000 *kurucs* of Thököly and Wesselényi, who had temporarily patched up their differences. Keen to press on after the capture of Hadjúböszörmény and Nagykálló, Thököly became frustrated by the confusion that characterised this motley army, and after a furious row with Teleki, rode off in a rage.

Sensing that Leopold was now vulnerable on both strategic flanks, Thököly renewed his demands, including pardon for himself and his followers, religious freedom throughout Hungary and, finally, the hand of Helena. Aware that Thököly now had some 25,000 men under arms operating with impunity out of Transylvania, and given that the Turks had made peace with the Russians in February 1681, Leopold had to buy time since he could not switch his forces from the West, given that war with France was a certainty. He therefore consented to Thököly's marriage to Helena. In return Thököly agreed to an armistice. Financially, Leopold was the loser since his assent had cost him the income from the Rákóczi estates.

In the spring of 1682, Louis was up to his usual mischief, egging Thököly on by promising him 500,000 livres tournois if he took up arms again. By now, the Turks had abandoned the Ukraine and left Kiev to the Russians. Thököly's envoys were told he had the full backing of the Porte as Kara Mustafa had never let the prize of Vienna out of his sight—an attack was, for the Porte, merely a question of timing. When Thököly visited Paşa Ibrahim in Buda, he was cheered and hailed in the streets as "The King of Hungary". Handsome, tall, with flowing brown hair and luxuriant whiskers, he was eloquent and persuasive, the perfect foil for the Turks. Vienna, unaware of Kara Mustafa's intentions, continued its policy of conciliation: on 15 June 1682, a representative of the Emperor attended the marriage ceremony of Thököly and Helena.

The wedding festivities at Mukachevo lasted three days. The groom was 25, the bride 38. By the end the guests had consumed ten bulls, 36 lambs, 20 pigs, 80 sheep, 800 lbs of fish, two tons of honey; as well as 130 barrels of red wine and 150 of white, 40 barrels of beer and 25 of best Polish vodka. As for the troublesome Countess Zsófia, she had died two years earlier. Nine days after the wedding, Thököly broke the armistice and seized three important towns in Upper Hungary.

That summer, the Imperial Ambassador to the Porte, Count Caprara, reported to Vienna that the Sultan was obstructing the negotiations to renew the Treaty of Vasvár, which was coming to the end of its term. In his opinion, it was clear that the Porte had another agenda. Thököly, having concluded a treaty with Paşa Ibrahim, raised the standard of revolt throughout Upper Hungary. Now officially recognised as an Ottoman vassal, Kara Mustafa granted him royal status and in August sent a crown in the name of the Sultan, although even Thököly had the sense to refuse the title King of Hungary. He settled for Prince of Central Hungary. There was as always a price to pay; in this instance, the Ottoman terms were 40,000 thalers a year. The Prince of Transylvania, Mihály Apafi, was ordered by the Porte to break off negotiations with Vienna and to send troops to Hungary to fight the Imperial army.

Leaving her children behind, Helena followed her new husband on campaign. When she had to remain at home, she wrote letters of great passion:

"May God spare me from the fate of living even in the safest of castles without my most beloved husband. I do not want it; it is for me a question of life and death. No misery can make me falter in my attachment to you. Would that you could stand fast by me! I am ready to go to you, even by foot, wherever you may happen to be. What a great thing true love has been, so my sweetest darling, we should rejoice together when fate smiles on us; and should misfortune becloud our sky, we should find consolation in sharing it with each other. Then we shall carry our cross together...."

With help from Paşa Ibrahim, Thököly occupied Fulek and Košice. Hungary was on the point of reunification, but as an Ottoman protectorate —therein lay the flaw to Thököly's plan. At the zenith of Thököly's career as *kuruckirály* (King of the Rebels), the Estates at the Diets of Košice and Tallya now refused to finance him, concerned that the worthy goal of independence from the Habsburgs had been compromised by an unworthy dependence on a Turkish alliance.

Still Leopold sought conciliation and extended the truce, leaving Thököly unmolested. Finally in December, the true position of the Porte and Thököly was revealed to Leopold. There was to be no renewal of Vasvár unless the Imperial fort at Leopoldov was raised to the ground, a number of towns near Nové Zámky surrendered and Thököly recognised as King of Upper Hungary, which was to be under Turkish suzerainty. The note conveying this to Vienna read: "We declare to you that the Count Thököly and some Hungarian Lords, forced by the bad treatment you have a long time shown them, violating the Rights and Privileges of the Kingdom, have rendered themselves our Tributaries and annexed their country to our Empire. Therefore we request you after notice given that they are under our Protection, to restore them their Estates, if you would not break the Truce and draw on you the Punishment your rashness shall deserve."

This was nothing less than a declaration of war. While Austria digested this unwelcome news and sent a reply that Ottoman law did not authorize the 'Protection of Rebels', the Sultan and his Sadrazam set off from Edirne on 30 March 1683 at the head of the imperial Ottoman army. Despite atrocious weather, they arrived at Belgrade in the first week of May, where after agreeing that the first objective was the capture of Györ, the Sultan handed over command to Kara Mustafa. Joined by the Crimean Khan and Thököly en route, the Sadrazam encamped at Györ where he decided it was too well defended. Instead, he gave orders for the army to advance to Vienna. When news of this change of plan reached the Sultan in Belgrade, he was powerless to countermand it.

Suddenly Western Europe found itself once more threatened by a major Ottoman invasion. France, England, the Netherlands, Brandenburg and Spain sat on the sidelines for reasons of self-interest, but Pope Innocent XI managed to rally his German flock, with the German Diet voting money and Bavaria, Saxony and Brunswick-Luneburg sending men to fight. More importantly, Jan Sobiewski of Poland pledged a force of 40,000 men. Professor David Angyal wrote of Thököly at this crucial stage: "He could pilot his ship very cleverly on the sweet waters of the Hungarian—and Transylvanian—politics, but when his craft reached the sea of European policy, he was stranded. The idea of the attack on Vienna was not his idea, but he urged Kara Mustafa to undertake the enterprise. He wished to keep the Turks off Hungarian territory, and he had a firm belief, that supported by the Turks, he could take possession of the whole of Hungary, and be elected King of Hungary, and force Leopold to acknowledge the royal power thus acquired."

As the Turks massed for their attack on Vienna, prayers were offered to Allah: "Blow us with thy mighty Breath like Swarms of Flies into their Quarters, and the Eyes of the Infidels be Dazl'd with the Lustre of our Moon. Consume them with thy fiery Darts, and Blind them with the Dust which they themselves have raised." The bombardment of Vienna started on 14 July and, having installed "his fifteen hundred concubines guarded by seven hundred black eunuchs, amid gushing fountains, baths, luxurious quarters set up in haste but with opulence", Kara Mustafa told the Sultan that soon "all Christians would obey the Ottomans".

On 12 September under the overall command of Sobiewski, the relief of the city began. A contemporary report reads: "After a Siege of Sixty days, accompanied with a Thousand Difficulties, Sicknesses, Want of Provisions, and great Effusion of Blood, after a Million of Cannon and Musquet Shot, Bombs, Grenadoes, and all sorts of Fire Works, which has changed the Face of the fairest and most flourishing City in the world, disfigured and ruined most part of the best Palaces. In the Night the Christians made themselves Masters of all the Turks Camp." It had taken just eight hours.

The morning after the battle revealed bizarre sights. Sobiewski wrote to his wife: "The Rarities which were found in the Prime Vizor's Tent, were no less Numerous than Strange and Surprising, as very curious Parrots, and some Birds of Paradise, with all his Banios, and Fountains, and some Ostriches, which he Chose rather to Kill, than let 'em fall Alive into our Hands; Nay his Dispair and Jealousy transported him so far, as to Destroy his very Women for the same Reason."

Two days later, a service of thanksgiving was held at St Stephen's cathedral. Then came the bickering. The Elector of Saxony went home, irked that victory had been usurped by the Catholics; Leopold tried to upstage Sobiewski and claimed credit for the military triumph. In a letter home, Sobiewski wrote "we were treated as if plague stricken: everybody avoids us. It would have been proper, I think, to ask me how I propose to carry on the war; but no one says a word to me. Everyone is disheartened; we wish we have never helped the emperor, but that this haughty race had been eternally confounded." Louis XIV, brazen as ever, ordered the Marquis de Sébeville to congratulate the Emperor *"de l'heureux succès de ses armes"*. On the morning of 16 September, Leopold returned to Linz where he remained for the next ten months while Vienna was cleaned up.

Meanwhile, vital time was wasted, allowing the Ottoman army to retreat in relative good order. A week later the allies began advancing east in a campaign that would last for the next 16 years and bring to the fore Prince Eugene of Savoy, one of the great military leaders of his generation. Prince Louis of Baden presciently wrote of him to the Emperor, "This young man will with time occupy the place of those whom the world regards as great leaders of armies."

After their catastrophic defeat at Vienna, certain quarters of the Porte tried to blame Thököly. After all, his performance had been lacklustre; on reaching Bratislava, he had quickly retreated when confronted by the regular troops of Charles of Lorraine, and had refused to redeploy to Vienna when ordered by the Sadrazam. He considered pledging his stepson, Ferenc Rákóczi, as a hostage to the Sultan to prove his loyalty; Helena forbade it. Then, conspicuous by his absence from the Ottoman order of battle at the disastrous defeat at Párkány on 9 October, which led to the loss of the key Danubian fortress of Esztergom, he hastened to Edirne to defend himself before the Sultan. His erstwhile friend and commander, Kara Mustapha, was executed in Belgrade on Christmas day, strangled with a silk scarf and then decapitated. Heads rolled when defeat was visited on the Ottomans.

With the Turkish cause lost, Thököly offered terms to Leopold through Sobiewski. These were twofold. He would desist from rebellion if, first, the Emperor confirmed the rights of Protestants in Hungary and, second, he was granted the thirteen north eastern provinces of Royal Hungary with the title of Prince. The answer from Leopold was an emphatic 'No' and an unconditional surrender demanded instead. When the key mining town of Levoca was taken by Imperial troops on 10 December, Thököly's career appeared to have run its course. Abandoned by his men, cut off from his wife, outlawed by Vienna, the final curtain was slowly descending on the *kuruckirály*, who ignominiously took refuge at Debrecen behind the security of a strong Turkish garrison.

Sensing he now had the upper hand, Leopold used this opportunity to try and win over the remaining rebels. He set up an amnesty commission at Bratislava on 12 January 1684, published a decree promising to abide by the Sopron Diet of 1681 and offered free pardon and security of the estates of Thököly's former followers who presented themselves before the end of February to swear allegiance. In central and western Hungary, the response was excellent but in the north and east it was lukewarm. Trust in the Habsburgs was never lightly given.

Leopold now decided that despite continuing French hostility—Louis XIV had attacked Luxembourg at the same time as Vienna faced the Ottoman siege—the time had come to concentrate his forces in the East. Consequently he signed the Holy League with Poland and Venice to prosecute the war against the Porte in which no one power would sign a separate peace. It was to be a turning point in European affairs. A series of almost unbroken victories began with the successful siege of Nové Zámky and the investment of Buda.

In the winter of 1684, in keeping with his relentless character, Thököly renewed the war but was soundly defeated by General Schultz near Presov, losing his headquarters in the process. Undeterred and unaware that Mihály Apafi had signed a secret agreement with Leopold that spring, in which he recognised Leopold's suzerainty as King of Hungary and thereby in effect became a member of the Holy League, Thököly re-entered the fray in 1685. This time he was on his own—the Turks were besieged at Buda, while Louis XIV had agreed to a 20-year truce with Leopold. On 11 September, General Caprara's Imperial troops took Presov and by 13 October had surrounded Košice, forcing Thököly to flee into the safety of Turkish occupied territory.

Thököly once more decided to try and negotiate with Vienna, without the knowledge of the Turks. He sent a lieutenant, Stefan Szirmay, to Leopold after arranging for him to be 'captured' in an ambush near Samos. He promised Vienna that he would be a loyal servant of the emperor, break with the Turks, disassociate himself from the *kurucs* and deliver all the territory under his control to Leopold. The letter containing the offer represented an opportunity too good for the War Council to miss: if it fell into the hands of the Porte, it would surely destroy Thököly's standing with them once and for all. At the same time, if its contents were leaked to the *kurucs*, they would feel betrayed. The letter was duly forwarded to Muhammad IV and the young Szirmay incarcerated in the fortress of Graz, bringing his career as an envoy to an abrupt end.

After the pro-Ottoman Transylvanian Estates had confiscated Thököly's lands and imprisoned a number of his followers, the Turks, perhaps under the impression that Thököly could be traded with Vienna in exchange for favourable peace terms, decided to sacrifice their former ally. Paşa Ibrahim issued a warrant for his arrest and instructed the Paşa of Oradea to invite him to dinner on 15 October 1685. Thököly accepted. Seized, then bound and chained, he was delivered on a peasant's cart to Belgrade. Without soldiers, captains, territory or funds, Thököly lost all his military and political influence. His captivity immediately drove the remainder of the *kurucs* into the Habsburg camp, an own goal as far as the Sultan was concerned. Seventeen thousand *kurucs* gave their allegiance to Leopold who accepted their repentance in good faith; under Habsburg control, they now formed the basis of a regular standing army which could be deployed against the Porte. The Sultan ordered Ibrahim strangled and Thököly rehabilitated, then in January 1686 despatched to Transylvania with a small army. But it was too late: all but one of the key fortresses had fallen to the Imperial troops. Only the Rákóczi's Zamkova castle stronghold at Mukachevo remained holding out, with 4,000 of Thököly's *kurucs*, together with his family and diplomatic corps, who had sought refuge there the previous year.

In November 1685, the Aulic War Council ordered General Caprara, a relative of the famous Montecucculi, to capture this last remaining *kuruc* stronghold. Described as 'unenterprising, avaricious, envious and cruel, careless of the comforts of his soldiers, and never possessing their confidence', Caprara sent a letter to Helena, instructing her to surrender the castle, reassuring her that, if she broke with Thököly, he would spare her and her children. From this moment, Helena realized that the Habsburgs had not factored in the reaction of public opinion to their heavy-handed military solution. She quickly seized the propaganda initiative and replied that while she was not afraid of weapons, she hoped that the Emperor would not wage war on a woman who was protecting her children: setting the king's soldiers on widows and orphans was surely not a recognised custom of war.

During this exchange of letters, Helena and her castle captain, Sándor Gáspár, prepared to defend the castle to the last man. In military terms, her assets amounted to 4,000 troops and a formidable fortification, defended by three curtains of high walls and a wide moat. Her liabilities were a shortage of ammunition and supplies, limited funds and a mélange of refugees encamped within the castle precincts. Proceeded by a week of intense bombardment directed by the feared Italian mercenary General Caraffa, the siege of Mukachevo began in February 1686. Known for his statement, "If I believed I had in my whole body a single drop of blood favourable to the Hungarians, I would have my veins opened," Caraffa made a ruthless adversary. The attack did not go well: rainy weather, coupled with a shortage of ammunition, severely hampered the effectiveness of his artillery. On 9 March, Caprara sent Helena another letter, ordering her to surrender. She again refused, telling him she found it unbelievable that he was waging war against a mother and her two children. This was not the act of a glorious emperor or of his army's commander.

The Imperial army restarted their bombardment in earnest. This provoked Helena to order red flags flown from every turret as a sign of defiance. Her coolness under fire became legendary. On one occasion, a cannonball landed beside her and Ferenc as they walked along the battlements, killing a young maid who was following a few feet behind them. Helena continued her patrol in full view of the enemy. In late March, the Imperial forces directed their fire at Helena's personal living quarters, causing extensive damage to the buildings and killing her horse in the process. A 200-pound unexploded mortar bomb lodged itself in her bedroom.

By mid-April the Aulic War Council, alarmed by escalating costs and a rising tide of negative publicity, was exasperated by Caprara's failure to take the castle and ordered the siege commander, Caraffa, to rejoin the main army. A small contingent of cavalry remained behind to observe activities in the castle. On 30 April, the 10-year-old Ferenc Rákóczi rode out of the castle with a large escort to survey the scene. It was a moment of elation for the defenders. As they rode back up the hill, every cannon in the fortress fired a salute in honour of the young Prince and his mother. The defence of Mukachevo now symbolised the defence of Hungary. A month later, Ferenc and his sister Juliana led the celebrations for their mother's name day. Before a large crowd of soldiers and civilians gathered in the ruins of the bombed out castle, they offered a toast to Helena: "Blessed is this day and fortunate hour!"

Helena had indeed become the toast of Europe: Louis XIV pronounced her the reincarnation of Joan of Arc and sent her presents of jewellery; the Polish royal family wept tears of pride for her and in London, she was the Whig heroine of the day. Helena wisely used the respite to bring money, maize and other supplies from Poland and, on the diplomatic front, she sent envoys to Vienna and Paris to elicit continuing support.

However, the position of Mukachevo became increasingly isolated when, on 26 October 1686, Christian flags were raised over the ruined towers of Buda Castle by Charles of Lorraine's soldiers, signifying the end of 150 years of Ottoman rule in Hungary. News of this reached Mukachevo in a letter from Thököly. On 4 November, Helena sent an envoy to Sobiewski in Warsaw, requesting his help to ensure Hungarian interests were protected during this period of upheaval. But that autumn Imperial troops were once more redeployed to Transylvania and before long, Mukachevo was again blockaded.

The military picture was bleak. Although she had managed to re-supply and re-equip her forces, Helena knew that the continued long-term defence of the castle was impossible. The surrounding villages had either been ravaged by Imperial mercenaries or milked dry by their new German officer owners. Furthermore, Vienna now resorted to black propaganda to recover Mukachevo and accused Helena of cutting off the hands of prisoners of war.

Events began to overtake her. On 12 August 1687, at the second battle of Mohács, the Turks were soundly beaten by Charles of Lorraine and lost 30,000 men, leaving the way open for the Habsburg armies to invade all of Transylvania. Two months later on 27 October, as news of a widespread mutiny in the Ottoman army reached Cluj, the Prince and the Diet capitulated to Austrian demands. His deputy, János Haller, signed the Treaty of Blaj with the Austrians, handing over twelve major forts and making a cash payment of 700,000 forints to the Imperial army. The Prince was permitted to keep his title and the Estates retain their privileges, but Transylvania was now under the protection of Leopold. As Miklós Bethlen noted, "in a word, everything was now at the whim of His Majesty". Soon Habsburg troops arrived to garrison the western fortresses at Deva and Cluj. In the meantime, Thököly had been released from Turkish captivity and had made his way to Wallachia where he fought a series of minor skirmishes against troops from the Holy League.

A Hungarian Diet assembled at Bratislava on 18 October, at which the Estates recognised the Habsburg hereditary right to the Hungarian crown, the *ius resistendi* was repealed from the Golden Bull of 1222 and the Protestants' rights upheld. The crown of St Stephen was symbolically returned to Bratislava from Vienna and Leopold's son, Joseph, was crowned King of Hungary on 9 December.

These negotiations took place against a background of a renewed reign of Habsburg terror. As Professor Marriott wrote: "The Habsburg Emperor, now master of the whole of Hungary, proceeded to deal with his rebellious subjects and the embers of the insurrection were quenched in blood." General Caraffa's tribunals at Presov, approved by Leopold the previous year, were particularly notorious; he erected a scaffold, or 'slaughter-bank,' in the market-place where, from 20 February through to August 1687, a series of gruesome executions took place. Over twenty prominent citizens were tortured, decapitated or impaled, then drawn and quartered, their body parts strung up outside the city gates. Caraffa confiscated their lands and extorted huge amounts of cash from their families. In Debrecen, he imposed a crippling monthly tax of 80,000 forints, resulting in the use of extreme brutality to collect it.

In fairness to Vienna, as soon as it became clear that Caraffa had gone 'mad', the tribunal was scrapped and the scaffold dismantled. The general was reassigned to Sibiu and the excesses stopped. Curiously Leopold bestowed on him the Order of the Golden Fleece, a gesture which served to undermine the sincerity of the Emperor's public outrage. Nevertheless, fatal damage had been done to Transylvanian independence.

The Discontented: Love, War and Betrayal

On 8 November, Süleyman II deposed his brother the Sultan Mehmet IV, who had become obsessed by hunting to the exclusion of all forms of governance. The situation in Istanbul was far from stable. Siyanuş Paşa, the Sadrazam, when asked to pay the elite troops of the Janissaries, found the treasury empty; his body was cut to pieces by the unpaid soldiers and thrown out of the palace window. His wife and sister suffered similar fates. The next year, Süleyman in fear for his life, announced a move to Edirne, only to discover that there were neither enough horses nor money to move the court.

The days of Ottoman supremacy were coming to an end and throughout this period, Turkish defensive tactics proved flawed: by concentrating their forces on a handful of major fortifications, they allowed the smaller fortresses to be easily invested or bypassed, thus fatally weakening the integrity of their overall defensive line. Many once impregnable bastions, including Eger, Szekesfehervar and Szigetvár, fell without firing a shot.

The situation at Mukachevo was now desperate. No one had been able to leave the castle since the previous November and food and ammunition stocks were running dangerously low. Yet to prematurely relinquish it to the Imperial forces would remove Helena's only card—her international reputation as a latter day Joan of Arc. She wrote to Thököly and Sobiewski for help but none was forthcoming. At the end of 1687, she wrote to the French ambassador in Warsaw telling him that if she did not receive military assistance, she would have no choice but to enter into negotiations with the Imperial forces.

Realizing that the rebellion was nearly over, Thököly now proposed to the Pope that if his Holiness obtained advantageous terms for him from the Emperor, not only would he become a Catholic but also contribute to the persecution of the Lutherans. According to one contemporary source, he sent his letter in code to Helena for her comments; somehow she allowed it to fall into the hands of her chancellor, Dániel Absolon, a stalwart Protestant and former secretary to Prince Apafi. Appalled at Thököly's treachery, Absolon and the fortress commander, András Radics, deliberately squandered two months worth of supplies in a single week.

Thus on 17 January 1688, Helena had no choice other than to capitulate. The terms were not harsh: all the defenders were pardoned, she was allowed to keep her estates and those belonging to her Rákóczi offspring, but she had to take up residence in Vienna where the Emperor became the guardian of her children. Six days later, the valiant Hungarian garrison left Mukachevo, after a siege that had lasted for 813 days.

Helena arrived in Vienna on 27 March, on the twelfth birthday of her son Ferenc II. Three days later he was taken from her and sent to Bohemia to be educated as a Catholic. He was never to see his mother again. Accompanied by her daughter, Helena was retired to an Ursuline convent, where they both remained for the next three years.

The irrepressible Thököly obstinately refused to give up the cause of Hungarian independence. Nailed to every village tree, his Declaration of March 1688 read: "Ye People of Hungary, it is long ago since your Enemies and mine have published my Death, and nevertheless I am alive still, God be Thanked, to defend your oppressed liberty. How long will ye bear, ye brave Hungarians, their Triumph over your Innocence? If you had been designed to perish, is it not better to do it having your Arms in your hands, than to be put to death by an infamous hang-man? Make sane endeavours to get out of the shameful slavery wherein you are, seeing you want nothing else but the will to do it: the Power of your Enemies is not as great as you think." This last statement was typical of Thököly for he consistently underestimated the staying power of the Habsburgs.

As the historian László Konter points out, "his horizon of European politics was insufficient to demonstrate the vanity of his endeavour to shake off Habsburg rule in Hungary; but, ironically, it was his tragically mistaken Ottoman commitment in 1683 that catalysed the speedy realisation of what he envisaged as the next step: the liberation of the country from Turkish rule." Within months, on 8 September, Belgrade fell to the Habsburg armies after a desultory defence. The Elector of Bavaria easily overcame Thököly's covering force outside the city. The only light on the horizon for Thököly was Louis XIV's invasion of the Palatine, which once more meant that Leopold had to fight on two faraway fronts.

The peace initiative, started by William of Orange in 1688, whereby the Dutch offered to mediate between the Ottomans and the Emperor, had been making slow but sure progress. When the Anglo-Dutch Austrian alliance was signed in May 1689, the Sultan was on the point of accepting the Habsburg conditions for peace. Then Paris proposed a French-Ottoman alliance. Encouraged by the prospect of Imperial troop diversions to the western front, the Porte saw a chance to launch a major counter-offensive and make good some of their losses.

The long-serving Prince of Transylvania, Mihály Apafi, died on 15 April 1690. Thököly was immediately named Prince by Süleyman II, who was now advised by a new Sadrazam, Mustafa Köprülü, Ahmet's brother. The Habsburgs, who supported the Transylvanian Estates' nomination of Apafi's son, Mihály II, reacted by sending an army under the command of Generals Heister and Mihály Teleki to remove Thököly. In what should have been a straightforward engagement between the well-armed and well-trained Imperial forces and Thököly's rag-bag army of freebooters and mercenaries, a surprise lay in store. Thököly came up with an ingenious stratagem. As he headed north from Wallachia with his 6,000-strong army, he sent the Transylvanian contingent ahead on foot across the Carpathian Mountains, making sure they avoided the main paths and forest tracks. On 22 August, he surprised the Imperial army at Zarnesti, to the west of Brasov. Surrounded, they surrendered en masse and Thököly found himself with highly prized hostages in the persons of Generals Heister and Doria. Count Teleki, Thököly's mentor and former guardian, was killed.

His immediate response was to arrange a trade: the hostages for Helena. But circumstances, as ever, changed and the Sultan decided to keep them as insurance. There was no respite for Thököly: a month later he was forced to move on by Prince Louis of Baden. Once he had crossed over the Bodza Pass with the remnants of his army on 25 October, he was destined never to return to Transylvania. He again offered terms to Leopold—he would side with the Holy League if Vienna recognised him as Prince of Transylvania and honoured him with the title of a duke. Any agreement needed to be guaranteed by Venice and Poland. Nothing was heard from Vienna.

The Turks had counterattacked in the autumn of 1690 and, after recapturing Vidin, Mustafa Köprülü succeeded in retaking Belgrade on 8 October. Once more all the Austrian gains in Hungary were threatened, although there was also an unexpected bonus for Vienna. Over 200,000 Serbs, led by Patriarch Arsenije Cernojevic of Pécs, had migrated into Southern Hungary to escape the Ottoman army. This was to have lasting repercussions for the prospects of Hungarian independence since they were subsequently entrusted by the Habsburgs[1] with the entire southern defensive line. Signed on the expedient assumption that the Serbs would shortly return to where they had come from, the Privilege was never to be rescinded.

Leopold now tightened his grip on Transylvania. After meeting with Miklós Bethlen, the representative of the Transylvanian Diet, he issued the Diploma Leopoldinum on 16 October 1690, reaffirming the privileges of the three *natios*[2]15 and the special position of the accepted religions, within the framework of an autonomous province that reported directly to Vienna. There was to be no reunification of Transylvania with Hungary. He rejected the elections as Prince of both Thököly, the Ottoman nominee, and Mihály II Apafi, the Diet's nominee, and introduced an independent civil administration. In early 1691, the estates elected Count György Bánffy as Governor. Without the support of the Diet, Thököly was left high and dry in Transylvania, deprived of his estates, some of which had been mortgaged by his sister and others sold to Apafi.

In February, Helena, frustrated by her detention in Vienna, wrote to Thököly:

> "God bless your Lordship. I am able to write to your Lordship because General Heister Ephebus has come to me and asked me whether or not I would be willing to write to your Lordship. I was surprised that your Lordship had not written to me nor sent any news through the said Ephebus; but he excused your Lordship because no-one knew where they could get hold of you.
>
> Therefore I write to your Lordship that I am in good health, and I desire to know what my position is. Does my Lordship wish to abandon me or to recognise me as his wife? And to arrange my return to him through an exchange of hostages? For it will not be able to happen otherwise. May he be merciful, I

---

[1] The Serb Privilege of 1691.
[2] The three political constituencies of Transylvania—Saxons, Hungarians and Székelys.

ask, towards the prisoners, for I fear that something similar my happen with me.

In one word, I have committed myself to Almighty God and to your Lordship's love for me. A great thing between those who are married is true love and duty, in which I remain your Lordship's acknowledged spouse."

The long years of separation were beginning to take their toll.

During the summer of 1691 Mustafa Köprülü continued to lead his army westwards from Belgrade to Peterwardein, where he was intercepted by Prince Louis, who had hurried south after driving Thököly out of Upper Hungary. They met at the battle of Novi Slankamen on 19 August. The Turks were defeated and Köprülü killed. This massive but costly victory by Prince Eugene made the Ottomans' formal proclamation of Thököly as Prince of Transylvania on 22 September an empty gesture. Although Thököly had led the cavalry at Slankamen, his Turkish allies knew they had lost Hungary and Transylvania forever. It had been a disastrous year. The Austrians further consolidated their position by capturing Oradea in 1692 and then detained the young Prince Apafi in Vienna. He never returned home for Transylvania now governed by Austria no longer required a prince.

On Christmas Day 1693 a deal was finally signed in Vienna, whereby Thököly could exchange General Heister for Helena. The following spring, at Bačka Palanka on the lower Danube, his battle flags flying in the strong breeze, Thököly waited in high expectation, his men camped in the flowering meadows along the banks of the river. Escorted by a troop of Imperial cavalry, Helena dismounted from her carriage and embraced her husband for the first time in 11 years. Here they lived in some style, bankrolled by the French King, but the years of war and deprivation had taken their toll on Thököly. Wracked by gout, grey-haired and stooped, he looked to Helena for support and strength.

The Turks were unsympathetic to their former proxy and Defterdar Ali, the Grand Treasurer, summoned Thököly to Belgrade to warn him that only strong men were required to serve the new Sultan, Mustafa II. In 1695, under pressure from Vienna which still maintained an 8,000 strong army of occupation in Transylvania, the Sultan ordered Thököly and Helena to Constantinople, where they settled in Galata on a meagre allowance. So dire were their financial circumstances that they sold Helena's jewels and then bought an inn where the legates of the Transylvanian Princes had once lived. The news of Thököly as an innkeeper raised wry smiles in Vienna.

In 1697, Mustafa led his army back to Belgrade. Confronted by Prince Eugene at Zenta outside Timișoara on 11 September, the Ottomans were caught as they crossed the Tisza River: the Sultan with his cavalry and most of his artillery were already across on the left bank but the remainder of his artillery and all his infantry remained on the right bank, waiting their turn to cross the pontoon bridge. Although under orders from Vienna not to risk a battle, Eugene, with only two hours of daylight remaining, launched a ferocious attack. The result in Eugene's own words was a frightful bloodbath: the Turks broke ranks and a catastrophic defeat ensued with over 20,000 killed including the Sadrazam. Another 10,000 drowned in trying to cross to safety. The sultan escaped from the battlefield in disguise, leaving his entire supply column and war booty to the Imperial army. Eugene's losses were 300 killed and 200 wounded.

At the Peace of Karlowitz (Sremski Karlovci in today's Serbia) on 26 January 1699 the Turks led by Hüssein, the last of the Köprülüs, and the Austrians signed a treaty which began the process of disengagement after over 150 years of conflict. With the exception of the Turks retaining the Banat of Temesvar (Timișoara), the whole of Hungary reverted to Vienna; Podolia and Kameniec were restored to Poland and the Venetian conquests in Dalmatia and the Morea confirmed. Russia retained Azov for the duration of two years. Specifically excluded by name from the Treaties, on 24 September 1701 Thököly was sent to Gemlik, a village to the south of Istanbul. At least the cost of living was cheaper there and Thököly's health improved; his gout was cured, he went hunting and in 1702 he bought a summer resort two hours from the village.

Surrounded by her garden of roses, pomegranates and lavender, Helena died at Gemlik aged 59 on 18 February 1703, close to her beloved husband but five hundred miles from her son, Ferenc. She never knew of his renewal of the rebellion against the Habsburgs. "If she had known it," wrote Thököly to his stepson, "in her happiness, she would have been born again." Her tombstone read: "Here rests the pride and glory of her sex and her country after a life of heroic suffering".

After yet again flirting with conversion to Catholicism as a way to facilitate his passage home, Thököly recanted and reaffirmed his Protestant faith in September 1705. Shortly after, aged 48, he died. His secretary, Komáromy, arranged for him to be buried under a tree in the Armenian cemetery, since the Sultan had refused the repatriation of his body. On the simple gravestone, under the Thököly crest, his epitaph read: "*Bene sperando et male habendo transit vita*"—"Our life passes, hoping for good but experiencing evil."

Professor Lodge concludes: "In spite of his fiery courage, his persuasive eloquence, his constancy in misfortune, and the dramatic vicissitudes of his career, it is clear that his hatred of Austria which he inherited from his father was stronger than his devotion to the real interests of his country, and that his action on more than one momentous occasion was determined by personal ambition." Thököly could never bring himself to trust Vienna and hence could not negotiate with the Emperor in good faith. This made his diplomacy one-dimensional: his only feasible overtures and alliances were directed to the Porte, a limitation that was as unacceptable to the rest of Europe as it was to Vienna.

Thököly's remains were repatriated to Hungary in 1906. After a state funeral at the Lutheran Church in Deak Square in Budapest, he was finally laid to rest at the family seat in Kežmarok. A speech at the interment service on 30 October ended: "Leave now, wanderer, remember the deceased, and ponder that the heavens may be conquered only with such weapons."

Born into the crucible of dissent, Thököly was a worthy standard-bearer of Hungarian nationhood. If his political judgment was poor and his motives occasionally questionable, his courage and resilience in the face of extraordinary odds was unsurpassable. His military achievements may not have been spectacular but they turned the idea of rebellion, as espoused by Nikolai Zrinyi and the Magnates' Conspiracy, into a reality. This was the challenging legacy he left to the next generation of Hungarian patriots.

Chapter Four
Ferenc Rákóczi II

In 1688, when Leopold entrusted the education of young Ferenc Rákóczi II to Cardinal Kollonics, he thought he had effectively drawn a line under the treasonable activities of this troublesome family. Best remembered for his infamous one-liner—"I will make Hungary first captive, then poor, then Popish"—Kollonics was determined that his young charge would eschew the ardent nationalism of his father. At 15, Rákóczi enrolled as a student at Prague University under the supervision of a Jesuit priest, and his letters to his mother Helena, keenly read by the Emperor's spies, became a mere trickle.

In June 1691 his sister Juliana escaped the banishment of convent life by marrying General Aspremont, a man twice her age. Now through his intervention, she managed to secure Ferenc's emancipation. At 17, he was free to dispose of his property—almost 2,800,000 acres—and no longer required a guardian. In gratitude, he moved into the Aspremont Palace in Vienna and gave his sister half his estates. At the instigation of Juliana and with the connivance of Louis XIV, in September 1694, Rákóczi secretly married the beautiful 15-year-old Princess Charlotte-Amalie, the eldest of six daughters of the Duke of Hesse-Rheinfels.

The news was initially met with silence in Vienna; then an arrest warrant followed. As Rákóczi admits in his Memoirs, he had gone to Hesse on the pretext of visiting the Imperial troops stationed there without alerting the court of his marriage plans. However, since none other than the Bishop of Cologne had officiated at the wedding, the Emperor had to relent and withdrew the warrant. The newlyweds moved to the Rákóczi estate at Sárospatak, where neither spoke much Hungarian and were viewed disapprovingly by the locals as 'Germanized'. The only exception to this frosty reception was the warm welcome extended by Rákóczi's powerful neighbour, the politically ambitious Count Miklós Bercsényi, Governor of Ung County and Imperial Commissioner.

Three years later, a peasants' revolt broke out on the Rákóczi estates at Tokaj. Crowds at the annual fair killed the Imperial tax collectors and the small detachment of soldiers sent to guard them. At dawn on 1 July 1697 the rebels led by the mayor of Végardó village, occupied Sárospatak castle. Further south, former soldiers of Thököly's *kurucs*, seized the castle of Tokaj. A great cry for the return of the *kuruckirály* went up. Rákóczi, in Vienna at the time, hurried to the *Hofburg* to assert his loyalty to the Emperor. Probably put up to it by Amalie, he suggested swapping his estates for some of similar value in Austria or Germany. The Emperor declined the offer and encouraged him to return to Hungary. In the meantime, the rebellion had been swiftly suppressed by Imperial forces; at Sárospatak, thirty culprits were executed on the spot.

Conditions in Hungary continued to deteriorate. The war of the Palatine Succession and continuing hostilities against the Ottomans were costing the Emperor 20 million forints annually. For example, in the Imperial Decree of 24 December 1698, the court set the annual tax in Hungary at 4 million florints in cash, of which about 600,000 florints was to be found by the nobility and free cities, the remainder by the Hungarian people. This was twice the annual levy of the previous five years. Taxation consequently became exorbitant, with taxes on consumption and inheritance, a tax in kind to support the army, a turnover tax levied on bees, wine, brandy and meat; add to these the Imperial monopolies on silver, salt and cattle and the popular expression of the time makes sense, "the Germans do not leave any udder of the cow un-milked."

The palatine, Pál Eszterházy, wrote several memos to the Government in Vienna. "What is good for you in the liberation of our country if you will rule over deserted forests and mountains?" A feudal tenant had to pay 47 different taxes, which left him with approximately 18% of his income. In addition, the cost in kind of provisioning the occupying Imperial army-about 40-50,000 foreign soldiers were now billeted in Hungary-was ruinous. Many families fled to the woods and joined the *bujdosok* and the remnants of Thököly's *kurucs*. The Imperial General Kopp von Neuding hung non-payers from the trees in the forest of Czenk.

Resentment of the 1687 Diet of Bratislava was deeply ingrained in Hungarian political attitudes, particularly the loss of rights to take up arms against the King in the event that the freedoms of the nobility were violated (the *ius resistendi*) and the abolition of the Hungarian's right to elect their own King. Now add the activities of the *Commmissio Neoacquistica* under Leopold's Grand Chamberlain, Prince Dietrichstein, whose brief was to validate claims of former owners of property in ex-Ottoman territory, and the situation became explosive. Far from being fair and open, the commission rented land to the Imperial nobility, rewarded those loyal to Vienna and sold off the surplus at market prices. Even for those whose claims were accepted, they had first to validate them (almost impossible after 150 years of war) and then pay an indemnity of 10% of the value of the land, which many could not afford. Others, falsely accused of siding with Thököly, saw their lands confiscated.

The Habsburg policy of settling thousands of Serbs and Germans ("Swabians") along the military frontier in Hungary and in Transdanubia with preferential tax breaks only exacerbated ill feeling. These settlers were indebted to Vienna, who exempted them from billeting and other military impositions. The Serbs were competent and hardy soldiers, excelled in mobile warfare and could field 40,000 men to fight the Imperial cause. To aggravate these nationalistic wounds, the German-based Order of Teutonic Knights received large landholdings between the Danube and the Tisza rivers.

Furthermore, Vienna had refused to acknowledge the role played by Hungarian troops in the war of liberation against the Turks. Since 1682, when Leopold had reconstituted the Hungarian army, an average of 13,000 troops had been engaged on active service each year. From 1683–1690 expenses amounted to 96 million forints, out of which Hungary had to pay a third without any share in the spoils of war, the traditional 'offset' arrangement. Not one Hungarian had been invited to the Peace of Karlowitz in 1699.

Thus, it was only a matter of time before Rákóczi became the centre of resistance to the Habsburgs. His initial reluctance, perhaps stemming from his disrupted and chaotic childhood, was soon dispelled by his best friend Count Miklós Bercsényi, who "awakened his sense of princely calling and responsibility to his country[1]16". He put out feelers to France and Poland for support to throw off the Austrian yoke.

---

[1] Kontner.

In Transylvania, the position of Governor was being undermined by Habsburg commissioners—Bánffy was stripped of his castle and salaried staff—and all Transylvanians removed from tax collection positions. One Imperial official, Count Seau, was quite often drunk after lunch and frequently disgraced himself by taking pot shots at *kuruc* prisoners who were being held in the yard at the castle of Alba Julia. Attempts to persuade the Emperor to reconsider an independent Transylvania came to nought.

In 1699, the French ambassador in Vienna, the Duc de Villars, a remarkable soldier and diplomat, approached Rákóczi with a view to organizing a general uprising. By the following autumn, the deterioration of the situation in Upper Hungary and prospect of a war in the west between Louis and Leopold convinced Rákóczi that now was the time to act. He wrote to Louis XIV on 1 November as "a father and protector" and offered his services.

His letter was intercepted by the Austrian authorities who captured its courier, Captain Longueval, at Linz and forced him to work for them. Although warned by his sister that Versailles's reply was now in the hands of the Emperor, Rákóczi had no time to escape: on 19 April 1701, two officers seized him at his castle at Sárospatak, put him in fetters and took him to Vienna where he found himself in the same prison cell as his grandfather, Petar Zrinyi. He even found his inscription scratched on the wall: "A man who is just and clings faithfully to his goal cannot be deterred by the face of the tyrant who persecutes him." The gossip in Vienna had it that Amalie was having an affair with Longueval and had no objections if her husband was executed.

In reality, Amalie, pregnant and unwell, rushed to Vienna to mobilize her connections, while Bercsényi managed to evade arrest and crossed over to Poland. After six weeks in prison, in early November 1701, Rákóczi managed to escape with the help of the prison commander, Captain Lehman, who had been persuaded by a Jesuit priest, Father Wolf, and Amalie that he should facilitate the escape. She also offered him an inducement of 30,000 forints. Lehman gave Rákóczi a Dragoon's uniform and escorted him past the prison wardens to a house where a saddled horse awaited him. Rákóczi managed to bluff his way past the officer on guard at the city gates just as they were closing and rode off into the night. Lehman was subsequently court-martialled, found guilty of treason and executed. When he reached Poland, Rákóczi learnt that Amalie had given birth to a son.

On his arrival in Poland, Rákóczi made contact with Prince Adam Sieniawska, Paladin of Belz, whose castles at Moscsenicza and Berezhany was close to the border. Here he was offered refuge and soon won the affections of the Paladin's wife, Princess Elizabeth Sieniawska, who allegedly became the great love of his life. The leader of the pro-French party in Poland, Elizabeth brought her considerable political influence to bear on the case for Hungarian independence. With their Hungarian estates confiscated and a high price on both their heads, Rákóczi and Bercsényi had no time to waste and renewed their contacts with the French through the Marquis du Heron in Warsaw. Their first request was for additional funding since the finance provided by Louis to date was in no way sufficient to start a serious and sustainable campaign.

Tamás Esze, a salt trader of Tarpa, and Albert Kis, a fugitive serf, joint leaders of the *bujdosok*, now approached Rákóczi to start a general uprising but he deemed it premature. As he set about canvassing international support, his plan was straightforward but by necessity ambitious. Sultan Ahmet III had made it clear to the French ambassador that he was not interested in siding with France and the *kurucs* against the Habsburgs: he would rather sit back and watch the infidels fight each other. Rákóczi's first call therefore was on Leopold's European enemies, France and Bavaria; then the neutral states, Poland, Sweden and Russia, who were all engaged in their Great Northern war for the Baltic, and finally the Protestant allies, England, the United Provinces and Brandenburg Prussia. Unlike Thököly, Rákóczi was a devout Catholic as were most of his commanders, but with 90% of his troops Protestant, he was able to claim that Hungary was fighting only to protect all its religions and its freedom. The drawback to this line of argument was that when the English and Dutch envoys to Vienna raised the issue of ill-treatment of Protestants, the Habsburg officials in turn raised the subject of English persecution of Catholics in Ireland. The outcome of all these approaches was disappointing since only the French expressed support.

Rákóczi's caution approach proved to be correct. Soon, the Aulic War Council in Vienna ordered the withdrawal of nearly all the Imperial troops from Hungary, who were urgently needed in the west for the War of the

Spanish Succession. On paper Leopold had around 135,000 men under arms, but in fact they amounted to only 74,000, of which 34,000 were in Italy and 28,000 in Germany, leaving only 4,000 in various garrison towns in Hungary. In addition there was a security force of 8,000 based in Transylvania under the unpopular General Rabutin, who had reputedly "been driven from France by lechery and murder, so in Vienna a dishonourable marriage and acquisitiveness had promoted him to everything and even to the command in Transylvania."[2]

Furthermore, Vienna faced a financial crisis. The Imperial banker Oppenheimer had initially informed the Emperor that financing Eugene of Savoy in Italy was all he was prepared to do. In May 1703, shortly after Oppenheimer's death, confidence in the bank collapsed, leaving Vienna, indebted to the bank to the tune of 15 million forints, so desperate for money that they had to sell the Turkish prisoners in Buda back to the Porte for a mere 170 forints. There was no money to pay the armies in Italy or the Empire.

After the surrender of Mukachevo by Imperial troops in February 1703, on 6 May Rákóczi and Bercsényi issued the Proclamation of Berezhany calling on all Hungarians to take up arms against the Habsburgs. In particular, they focussed on the grievances of the nobility, without whose support they would be unable to proceed. His supporters, however, had jumped the gun; they foolishly attacked country houses, thereby alienating the very nobility that Rákóczi was trying to woo. The uprising was quickly crushed by the loyalist Baron Sándor Károlyi. Having crossed the border into Hungary on 16 June, instead of the disciplined force he hoped to find waiting for him, Rákóczi encountered a motley group of 300 peasants, armed with pitchforks and scythes.

After this unimpressive start, the force soon swelled to 8,000 but they were still mainly untrained peasants. Only about a quarter were armed with old fuse-ignition muskets, the remainder with cheap sabres. In an early encounter with Károlyi, Rákóczi had to scurry back over the border into Poland and sit it out in the village of Závadka. Providentially, Bercsényi arrived with money from France and six companies of Polish Wallachian

---

[2] Miklos Bethlen.

dragoons, experienced and well-trained fighting men.

Delighted to see the Hungarian rebellion revived under a charismatic new leader, Louis subsidised the new insurrection with 50,000 livres tournois a month until 1708—but this covered only a fraction of the cost of financing an eventual total fighting strength of 70,000. To compensate for the deficit, Rákóczi founded a private mint and used his own silver and gold plate for making coins. Wine from his Tokaj estate was sold as far away as Danzig—a good bottle retailed at today's price of US \$160—the family jewels and suits of armour were sold off and his salt mines in the Maramures worked overtime.

After receiving assurances from Rákóczi in the Nameny manifesto of 18 July that he would safeguard their ancestral rights, the nobility came on side, although Rákóczi's Patent of Vetés on 28 August, which exempted armed surfs from feudal dues, was less well received. By the end of the year about half the kingdom, including the important mining towns of Zvolen, Levoca and Kremnica in northern Hungary, was under *kuruc* control. Louis XIV sent 100,000 livres tournois as a further contribution.

In November, Baron Sándor Károlyi, the Imperial general, switched sides and came over to the *kuruc* camp; his earlier victory over the rebels at Dolha, near Mukachevo, had been dismissed in Vienna where he had been accused of exaggerating the *kuruc* threat. Károlyi now became commander of the *kuruc* army. His second in command, Colonel Bottyan, was famous for his daring exploits; as a young man, he had infiltrated the Ottoman-held fortress of Nové Zámky and climbed the minaret where he threw the muezzin off the balcony as he called the faithful to prayer.

Rákóczi knew that the only feasible strategy for the liberation of Hungary was through meaningful military victories against the Habsburgs. Only through these victories would the international community take Hungary seriously, and likewise force Leopold to relinquish his claim to the Hungarian throne. Initial success came with the capture of Kallo and Debrecen and the defeat of General Count von Schlick at Altsohl. Rákóczi's horsemen roamed the plains of the Danube at will, while the Emperor's men sat tight in the fortresses of Nové Zámky, Leopoldov, Košice and Presov. The fortress of Eger, a symbol of heroic resistance against the Ottomans, surrendered to the *kurucs*.

The Discontented: Love, War and Betrayal

By January 1704, the *kuruc* army had grown to around 70,000 men, organised into two infantry regiments of 1,200 men each and one cavalry regiment of a 1,000; the remainder had yet to be trained. In February, Rákóczi, together with Bercsényi, issued a manifesto in Latin and French, beginning their appeal with twenty-one points to remind the world of Hungary's grievances. Leopold is said to have fainted when he read it. At the same time, Louis's ally, the Elector of Bavaria, invaded the Tyrol, captured Passau and headed for Linz.

This apocalyptic scenario, masterminded by the French, in which Vienna simultaneously faced a serious military threat in the west and an equally serious political and military threat in the east, was the stuff of Habsburg nightmares. It was time to talk. When Rákóczi met with Archbishop Széchényi in March at Gyöngös to start negotiations with Vienna, neither side could agree on the preliminaries. Leopold wanted his son, Archduke Joseph, to act as intermediary; Rákóczi insisted on the experienced Anglo-Dutch diplomatic team of George Stepney and Jacob Jan Hamel-Bruynincx.

From the beginning, the Anglo-Dutch team was regarded with suspicion by Leopold's advisers. Bruynincx, arriving in Vienna from Bratislava on 15 March, brought with him a letter from Bercsényi. The *kuruc* demands were clear: to have the *kuruc* forces treated as "Free States", for Rákóczi to be recognised as their 'chief' and for sufficient security guarantees to be put in place. Shortly afterwards a letter fell into the hands of Stepney, outlining a plan whereby the Elector of Bavaria and Rákóczi intended to besiege Vienna that spring. Concluding that this was impossibility since General Heister and his army lay between the city and the *kurucs*, Stepney did nothing. Curiously, almost immediately, a whispering campaign started against Stepney in the Imperial court; he was seen to be too close to the rebels and too friendly with Rákóczi's sister, the Countess Aspremont. The latter sleight was absurd in that the Countess had been his next-door neighbour at the Palais Lamberg for the last four years and was popular and well-liked by Viennese society.

Even with the promise of Anglo-Dutch guarantees, Rákóczi felt uneasy about the enforcement of any settlement. He replied to their letter of 22 April 1704, in which they set out a framework for discussion, by pointing out that "I do not see how the acceptance of a mediation in this kingdom can be accepted, the States and Orders of the Kingdom having not yet declared any intention to treat, from which I fear they may be wholly alienated by the exorbitancies of the Imperial Army, the burning of villages, ravaging the people and the horrid murdering of children. We are invited to treat of a Peace without sincerity, which has been [failed] to us by the violation of the Royal word and agreement."

Stepney took up the issue of infant deaths with Archbishop Széchényi, who told him that he had heard similar stories of soldiers roasting children but he suspected the Rascians[3]18. In turn the Archbishop took up these complaints with the Emperor, and added a few of his own since Austrian troops had ransacked his churches. The reply came back that the Aulic War Council had a very different version of events, endorsed by the Emperor, namely that these excesses were committed by the *kurucs*, not by Imperial forces. In May, a Deputy from the Reformed Churches of Transylvania arrived with news that students and professors had been massacred by Imperial forces at Engodin. When Bruynincx mentioned this together with the burning of 200 Transylvanian villages to Prince Eugene, he was told it was a pity that the number had not been 2,000 for 'as much as that whole people was Rebellious.'

Aside from bloody confrontation with the Habsburgs, Rákóczi's rebellion caused rifts within many Hungarian families. Take the Andrássys, originally from Transylvania. Nicholas Andrássy had distinguished himself as a soldier under Montecucculi's command in 1664 and his son, Peter III, unflinchingly served Vienna during Thököly's rebellion. However his six brothers were devoted supporters of Rákóczi, with Stefan and György Andrássy both rising to high rank in the *kuruc* army. Similarly, the Forgách and Csáky families were both pillars of the Habsburg establishment, yet both produced prominent rebel commanders.

In certain ways, Rákóczi was a revolutionary rather than a rebel leader. He wanted to modernise Hungary's government and reform its outmoded feudal systems. Only by unlocking its potential, he argued, could Hungary rejoin the European top table, which it had been so abruptly forced to leave in 1526. He relished the prospect of transcending the old social divides and uniting the country from within.

---

[3] Serbian troops from Southern Hungary.

The Discontented: Love, War and Betrayal

With their genius for administration, Rákóczi and his key team of Bercsényi and General Forgách (who had switched sides in April 1704), modelled their army on the French system, establishing gun foundries, munitions and uniform factories, and setting up food and supply depots. By 1706, huge progress had been made in training the *kuruc* army, now organised into 30 infantry and 45 cavalry regiments, mainly made up of Hungarians but also Slovaks, Ruthenians and Wallachians. An elite company of nobles provided his special forces while France seconded to him a group of professional artillery and engineering officers. The talented Colonel La Riviere built Ersekujvar fort for Rákóczi and on several occasions threw major bridges over the Danube and Tisza rivers. French commanders were also to be found in the front ranks of the infantry—Fierville d'Herrissy, Baron Vissenaque, Charriere, d'Absac, Despignon and Norwal all served with distinction.

In March 1704, the commander of the Imperial troops, the obstinate and brutal General Heister defeated Károlyi near the Raab River. In true *kuruc* tradition, Károlyi countered with a lightning raid towards Vienna and burnt down the Emperor Maximilian's palace at Kaiser-Ebersdorf. General Herberstein then arrived from the south with his Serbian levies but not before the *kurucs* had inflicted a crushing defeat on General Rittschau at Szomolány on 28 May, leaving the way open into Moravia. Together with the Ban of Croatia, János Pálffy, the Imperial generals managed to regain the initiative and, aside from a daring raid by Károlyi when he devastated the enormous Neugebaeude Schloss on the Emperor's birthday, in the process capturing his two favourite leopards, there was little progress by the *kurucs*.

Such defiant acts were little more than gestures of bravado. On 13 June, 7,000 Hungarians under the command of General Forgách were soundly defeated by General Heister at the battle of Koronco, south west of Győr. 3,000 kurucs were killed compared to the relatively light casualties of 150 Imperial troops. It was a serious setback.

In early July, Rákóczi was elected Prince of Transylvania by the Estates at Alba Julia, a rebuff for the Emperor who considered the Principality as an integral province of Austria. This election strengthened Rákóczi's international reputation though Louis XIV never acknowledged his sovereignty as a Prince. However the situation in Transylvania remained precarious; on 16 July, Miklós Bethlen wrote to Stepney in Vienna, complaining about "rough treatment from Count Rabutin."

On 13 August 1704 Louis suffered a major defeat at Blenheim (Hochstadt) in the War of the Spanish Succession. As C.A. Macartney wrote "any hope that it (the rebellion) would end in giving back Hungary its full independence vanished on the day Marlborough's victory at Blenheim destroyed the vision of French and Hungarian soldiers meeting in the streets of Vienna." Soon after, Pope Clement XI, in a Counter-Reformation mood, warned Louis "not to give any support to [Rákóczi] the mortal enemy of the church"; after all, his *kuruc* forces were 90% composed of Protestants. This was a blow since until then Rákóczi had relied on French support. At the same time, news of Thököly's death arrived at the Prince's court.

Peace negotiations continued. The indefatigable Anglo-Dutch team had managed to persuade the Habsburgs to accept eighteen of Rákóczi's Twenty One points; the outcome of the negotiations now depended on the resolution of the remaining three. The *kuruc* cause was not helped by General Forgách publishing a "virulent Patent" in Croatia, urging the population to rise up against the Emperor nor were matters made easier by the posturing of the Imperial team, which included Baron Seilern, who according to Stepney "could not be more odious" to the Hungarians. Likewise, reports from the Island of Rabau describing General Heister as exercising "great cruelties" were followed a few weeks later by the news he had impaled the *kuruc* commandant of a nearby fort. On 3 September, Bruynincx and Stepney managed to gain an audience with the Emperor and asked him to restrain his over-zealous general. One unexpected result of this meeting was that the Imperial go-betweens were changed and the new president of the Conference, Prince Liechtenstein, with his estates bordering Hungary, had a vested interest in broking a peace.

Prince Eugene and the Bohemian Chancellor Wratislaw, the architect of the alliance between the Emperor and the Maritime Powers, continued to express reservations about Stepney to the Emperor. Leopold wrote to Wratislaw in a letter dated 4 October: "On my part I would have fain have gotten out of the Hungarian affair long ago, but these turbulent people demand such insolent and audacious things, have also sought ways and means to promote their ends, that it is impossible to blindly assent to them.

About these circumstances I charge you accurately to inform Marlborough, and to assure him that I will willingly do all which is possible to facilitate this work, but Stepney has always shown too much passion in the matter…While I really cannot say what cause he has had, I can say that at certain times and occasions he has gone and been carried away too far in his expostulations, that it almost seemed as if he would inflame the rebels instead of helping to bring them to reason."

A tentative truce was arranged by Bishop Széchényi in October at Banská Stiavnica where Stepney and Bruynincx acted as observers but nothing came of it as, at the last minute, Vienna demanded the cession of a hundred square miles of Hungarian territory. Rákóczi wrote in exasperation "the true intention of the Imperials was to widen the breach rather than to heal it." Although the *kurucs* took the towns of Košice and Presov in October and Nové Zámky in November, a further Conference was held on 26 December. Stepney and Bruynincx explained to Prince Liechtenstein and Baron Seilern that, when they had met with Rákóczi at Bad Eisenbach in November, they had told him in most explicit terms that he would never be acknowledged by the Emperor as the Prince of Transylvania and that he had not raised the matter again in the course of their seven hour meeting.

Little did they know that the *kurucs* had just suffered a setback in an encounter with General Heister at Trnava on Christmas Day. Instead of prosecuting the battle, Rákóczi's infantry started looting the Imperial supply train, which had become sandwiched between the two front lines. When one of his German infantry regiments switched sides, Bercsényi noted: "We have beaten the Germans and confusion has beaten us." This was somewhat of an understatement for Heister's 11,000 men had undoubtedly got the better of Rákóczi's 22,000.

In desperation, Rákóczi despatched Pál Ráday, his chancellor, to revive the Hungarian-Swedish alliance, based on his commitment to uphold Protestant rights and religious freedom. But the day to day military problems remained the same for Rákóczi: inadequate military knowledge coupled with a shortfall of trained officers and soldiers, which, when combined with a chronic shortage of money and fluctuations in front line numbers, inevitably gave the advantage to the Habsburgs and their increasingly professional army.

Discipline remained a problem. After a raid into Moravia, Bercsényi wrote: "Against my strongest orders the soldiers, farmers and tartars destroyed like ants throughout the land. You could see their fires two miles wide...yesterday I saw three fires myself. They are such damn fools! I blush over the inability of our people to understand the consequences of their disobedience. They burn all the rich villages....they don't even plunder them!"

At the heart of all these difficulties was the fact that Rákóczi's army was a peasant army, motivated by deprivation rather than nationalism, and marked by distrust between soldiers and officers. It remained more or less as it had been under Thököly—a mass of peasant bands albeit this time organised into companies and regiments, unable to take on the Imperial forces and secure the strategic victory Rákóczi so desperately needed. The historian István Czigany estimates that "even the best-armed cavalry regiments were not satisfactorily equipped, since only 80–90% of the soldiers had swords, only 50% had pistols, and only 30–50% had guns compared with the Imperial Army, where the troops were fully equipped with firearms." Furthermore, with the feudal system of agricultural labour still more or less intact in Hungary and Transylvania, the nobility were ambivalent about their labour force being deployed on military adventures rather than on their landed estates.

The *kuruc* rebellion developed its own culture under the guidance of Rákóczi, who understood how music and poetry acted as the spiritual adhesive for good morale. Contemporary prints show *kuruc* soldiers relaxing to the sounds of tárogatós, an instrument similar to the clarinet. For reasons of prestige, he employed his own portrait painter, Adam Mányoki. His was a great talent of Baroque portraiture. His major works included portraits of Rákóczi in Hungary (1708) and Danzig (1712). Later on at the Hapsburg court, he painted portraits of Charles VI and his children.

During the winter months, Rákóczi had managed to take control of much of northern Hungary, which included gold and coal mines, saltpetre fields and cloth factories. A daring raid along the Danube as far as Schwechat just to the east of Vienna reminded the Emperor, as he watched the flames of the burning villages from his window, that the *kuruc* threat was as real as ever. By March 1705, Rákóczi's troops were in the suburbs of Bratislava.

This prompted Vienna to restart peace negotiations, with Stepney and Bruynincx, supported by the Imperial Count Harrach broking the idea of another armistice.

Events moved quickly. The French General, Des Alleurs, arrived as an intermediary on behalf of Rákóczi; on 11 April, General Heister was dismissed, a political sacrifice rather than a vote of no confidence in his military abilities. Then, on 5 May 1705, Leopold died.

His legacy was impressive. Not only had he doubled the size of the Habsburg territories but he had also established a world class army, both at the expense of the Hungarians. However, his advice to his son Joseph was wise: "Whatever the ministers say, make peace with the Hungarians. Demand the fulfilment only of the condition of the last Bratislava Diet and the right of inheritance; and whatever else the insurgents may demand, yield it, however hard it may appear; that you may then be able to protect the whole kingdom from foreign invasion."

Joseph I, a curious mixture of reformist and arch conservative, issued a manifesto on 14 May in which he stated his will to accede to all freedoms and rights of Hungarians. Stepney was convinced that Joseph had "positively resolved to examine into and redress the grievances which they (the Hungarians) suffered during his father's reign." Once more the Hungarians insisted that any such agreement must be guaranteed by external powers. Bercsényi reminded the Emperor that, as far as the Hungarians were concerned, the authority granted to him by the Bratislava Diet of 1687 had been obtained under duress. When Stepney and Bruynincx met in June with the Prince of Salm, the new Imperial First Minister, and Count Sinzerdorf, Joseph's recently appointed liaison officer to the Anglo-Dutch envoys, the idea of external guarantees for any Hungarian peace treaty was rejected. The view put forward by Prince Eugene that the rebellion was an internal affair had prevailed.

Sensing the need to maintain pressure on the new Emperor, Queen Anne despatched Marlborough's son-in-law, the Earl of Sunderland, to Vienna on 17 June. His instructions were clear: to urge the Emperor to come to an accommodation with Rákóczi since "the French avail themselves of this Diversion" and the ever-present danger of the Turk lurked in the east. The English and the Dutch would guarantee the 'performance of a treaty'.

Urging Sunderland to use his "best endeavours to put an end to the troubles in Hungary", the real agenda of the British was to focus the Imperial mind on the war against the French in Italy.

A daring *kuruc* raid into Moravia netted the rebels 400,000 forints and 300 breeding mares. The disconsolate owner, Prince Liechtenstein, appealed to Vienna, which gave him "permission to write to Prince Rákóczi to try if it be possible to buy them up of the Malecontents piece by piece at reasonable rates". On 9 July, the Emperor finally accepted the offer of Anglo-Dutch mediation and a flurry of diplomatic activity followed. A fortnight later, Stepney and Bruynincx proposed an armistice and detailed negotiations began on the exchange of prisoners.

Once more the peace process faltered. On 5 August, news reached the mediators that Joseph had ordered General Herbeville, with 16,500 Serbian and Danish troops, to leave his base on the Island of Schütt and march to Transylvania to relieve the besieged General Rabutin, who was battling to hold onto the fortresses at Sibiu, Brasov and Făgăraș with unpaid and unmotivated troops. This order effectively wrecked the peace talks for the Anglo-Dutch team's credibility was compromised: an Imperial army had marched, contrary to their assurances to the *kurucs* that it would not leave camp.

On 1 September, Rákóczi called for a national assembly at Szécsény on the Ipel, north of Vác, where a tented village soon sprang up in the open fields. Rákóczi opened the assembly by declaring that he was only there in his capacity as an individual nobleman and would accede to whatever decisions were made collectively. The assembly then declared itself a Confederation and placed Rákóczi in charge. He in turn created a State Council of twelve Councillors and a similar financial council; soon the vexed questions of religious freedom, relations with Transylvania and peace with Vienna had all been addressed.

The message to Vienna from Szécsény was clear: the Emperor was no longer dealing with one man but an entire nation. The Document of Federation read: "breaking with the unjustified aspirations for rule by the House of Austria, which disregarded all our laws and drove them into the ground, not only robbed our nation of its freedom but followed that with all imaginable cruelty....and we, with Duke Rákóczi having united our fatherland, take arms against the House of Austria which thirsts for our innocent blood." Victorious words were one thing, victorious actions another. Crucially, the assembly failed to free serfs from their obligation to work for their masters in time of war.

A formal peace-congress then met in Trnava that October with Wratislaw as the sole Imperial commissioner, but failed to make any headway, primarily because the *kurucs* still insisted on the independence of Transylvania. It would be a foolish Emperor who believed that the Transylvanian Princes would forsake their ties with the Ottomans when all recent evidence proved the opposite. Perhaps unfairly, Stepney pinned the blame for the failure of these talks on the Habsburgs, who by not consenting to the idea of an independent Transylvania, had laid "the Axe to the Root of the Tree and any man who has had the happiness of living under a free Government cannot but be a little concerned to see a poor people (where five parts of six are of the Reform'd Churches) depriv'd of their Liberties at one Blow."

After a long approach march lasting nearly three months, General Herbeville finally arrived in Transylvania and together with General von Schlick, defeated the *kurucs* at Jibou on 5 November. Rákóczi's 24,000 soldiers were out-fought by Herbeville's 20,000: the casualty figures were manipulated by both sides, with Vienna claiming it had inflicted 5,000 Hungarian casualties at a cost of only 500 of its own men. Harder to challenge were the statistics in a detailed report which reached Stepney: 17 canon and 2 mortars captured, 51 flags and standards left behind and Prince Rákóczi's personal baggage seized. However, after an emotional appeal to his soldiers—"My heroes, if there is Hungarian blood in your veins, and if there is a spark of love for me, your kinsman, left in you, revenge the grievous state of our honour and country"—Rákóczi ordered Colonel Bottyan to take control of Transdanubia, which he duly did in a brilliant lightning campaign, raiding far into the Austrian heartlands of Styria, thus counter-balancing the loss of Transylvania.

Marlborough had arrived in Vienna on 12 November by river from Ratisbon for a high level meeting with the Emperor and his advisors about the future prosecution of the war against France. Intrinsic to its planning was the question of money. Peace with the *kurucs* therefore took second place to these pressing matters about the future of Europe. With scant mention of the Hungarian problem, Marlborough left ten day later for Berlin in search of Prussian troops to help him carry on the war. Negotiations between Vienna and the *kurucs* limped on and when the Hungarian Confederates met at Miskolc in January 1706, Stepney and Bruynincx were desperately trying to tone down the draft declaration of the Emperor to his Hungarian subjects, for both feared it would do more harm than good.

On 13 April Rákóczi surprisingly requested a truce to begin in two days time and to last a fortnight. It may well be this was brought on by the worsening economic situation for price controls had been recently imposed by the Confederation's Economic Council. Wratislaw and Stepney promptly left for Bratislava and then continued to Trnava where they met with Bercsényi. Proposals were drawn up and the truce extended to 5 May. Suddenly there appeared to be progress and the Emperor consented to a concession that had been tabled two years previously: Princess Rákóczi was to be allowed to visit her husband. With her two sons, Jozsef and György, remaining in Vienna as hostages, and with assurances from Rákóczi that she would be returned whenever the Emperor decided, Amalie arrived at Bratislava in a brand new glass coach, drawn by six horses, with an escort of ten Imperial generals in full uniform and two squadrons of Imperial Dragoons. Here she was met by the *kuruc* "Prince of Fire", Brigadier Ocskay, a leopard skin pelisse slung over his shoulder, at the head of a cavalry detachment of troopers draped in wolf skins. Flags decorated the houses and church bells peeled as the entourage made its way to Nitra.

Stepney and Rechteren, the new Dutch mediator, arranged to meet with Rákóczi in his wife's apartment 'as if by accident'. They worked throughout the night and all through the following day, drawing up terms which were then forwarded to Wratislaw, who signed them with little alteration. The truce was extended until the end of July and after that, twelve days notice were required by either side to break it.

Throughout June and early July, frantic diplomatic activity continued between the parties. Carriages crammed with diplomats and messengers clogged the roads between Trnava, Bratislava, Nitra and Vienna. In return for peace, Joseph offered Rákóczi the principalities of Burgau in Swabia and Lichtenberg in Upper Franconia in exchange for dropping all his claims to Transylvania. Rákóczi refused and set three conditions: he would not relinquish the title of Prince of Transylvania; he wanted full independence for the principality, including the attendance of its Deputies at any peace conference; and any peace had to be guaranteed by foreign powers for the word and signature of a Habsburg Emperor were not to be trusted.

In the middle of these key negotiations, Amalie had left Nové Zámky to take the waters at Carlsbad. Her place was taken by Rákóczi's sister Juliana, Countess Aspremont, whom the Emperor had been 'pleased to employ.' She persuaded her brother to move to Šintava on the Váh River, which was only two hours journey from Trnava and thus easier to reach for the mediators and the deputies. At a meeting on 18 July, Rákóczi assured the mediators that he was ready to reply to the Emperor's last missive before the armistice expired. He was optimistic that reason would prevail and a deal was close to being hammered out.

It came therefore as something of a shock when two days later Stepney told him that there was little hope of the truce being prolonged and that the Emperor was adamant in his intention to govern Transylvania according to the terms of the Treaty of Karlowitz i.e. by a Governor and twelve Counsellors, all appointed by the Emperor. The mood in Vienna had swung to the hardliners who wanted to extirpate the Hungarians 'with fire and sword.' This may have been caused in part by the interception of a letter Rákóczi had written to Louis XIV in early March, from which it was clear that he was expecting an increase in the subsidy from France and also a declaration from Louis that he would consider supporting Rákóczi's claim to the Principality of Transylvania. Wratislaw warned Rákóczi: "Well, my Prince, you are putting your faith in France, which is the hospital of princes who have come to grief through her broken pledges and promises. You will increase their number and die there."

By 1 August, talks had collapsed and positions polarised. The armistice was lifted and war resumed. While it was clear to Rákóczi that the *kurucs* were not capable of inflicting a crushing defeat on the Imperial forces, militarily the situation remained promising for the rebels. They had reconquered most of Transylvania and were raiding across the western borders of Hungary. That month, General Rabutin again marched to northeast Hungary, while General Starhemberg, cousin of the great defender of Vienna Graf Rudiger Starhemberg, occupied Hungarian territories to the west of the Váh River. Rabutin then failed to prosecute the siege of Košice, losing many men in the process, and after marching west to assist Starhemberg in retaking south-west Hungary, only reached Buda in January 1707. This lacklustre performance of the Imperial forces stiffened *kuruc* morale and, in December, Rákóczi once more demanded the independence of Transylvania and the removal of Imperial troops as pre-conditions for renewed peace negotiations.

By now, many Hungarians had begun to ask what Rákóczi and his *kurucs* had really achieved. Liberty in a tenuous sense but certainly not prosperity. On 7 January 1707, the County of Turócz issued a circular letter, criticising Rákóczi for his 'imperiosity'. In a moment of uncharacteristic rage, Rákóczi imprisoned his close friend, General Forgách, for bringing him the bad news. The *kuruc* copper coins or *kongos* were valueless, poverty rife, taxes sky high and peace as elusive as ever. The previous year, the miners of Banska Stiavnica had sent a delegation to Rákóczi to complain about low pay. In March, they went on strike, demanding a wage increase and payment in silver coins. Discontent spread to Smolne where the miners rebelled in June.

Still searching for a way to make Vienna give ground, Rákóczi sent his secretary, Domokos Brernner, on a mission to Pope Clement XI in May. Brenner was told to stress Rákóczi's loyalty to the church and to ask the Pope to publicly support the uprising. His assent was also required for the nomination of the Bishop of Transylvania. The Vatican chose to ignore these overtures and continued to support the Emperor, formally disapproving of the insurrection and banning Catholic priests from any form of support to the rebels.

At the Diet of Onod, near Miskolcs, on 14 June, the representatives of the County of Turócz bluntly suggested that the present state of affairs was worse than under direct Habsburg rule. Bercsényi was enraged by this show of dissent and ran Rakovszky, the senior Turócz legate, through with his sword. The following day he presided over the execution of the second legate, Okolicsanyi. It was an inauspicious start to a meeting which went on to declare "we have learned how the Emperor Joseph usurped the throne, with the cruelty of a tyrant; we renounce our allegiance, and we deny Emperor Joseph the right to the Hungarian crown exacted from us by the House of Austria; and we declare that our country is without a King."

Rákóczi, as the elected Prince of Hungary, made no claim to the 'vacant' Hungarian throne since there was another prospect in the offing. David Corbea, the Wallachian diplomatic courier to Moscow, had been instructed by Peter the Great to offer Rákóczi the Polish Crown. In a replay of his grandfather György Rákóczi II's dream to unite Poland and Transylvania under the same ruler, the logic of the combined military and political clout of the two countries was compelling. Surely Vienna would respond with an offer to restore independence to Hungary. But it was a mere game, for Peter had neither the troops nor the money to impose such a scheme on the Poles and other interested parties. He had earlier that year told Mazeppa, the Cossack hetman, who had asked for urgent help against the Poles, "I cannot even spare ten men; defend yourself the best you can." By the autumn, Peter had lost interest in Rákóczi as Charles XII's armies threatened St Petersburg and Moscow.

The Diet of Onod failed Rákóczi miserably on three important counts. First, it destroyed the credit he had so painstakingly built up with the Protestant sea powers of England and The Netherlands. Second, out of loyalty to Sweden, Louis refused to ratify the Treaty of Warsaw, thus leaving him diplomatically isolated. Thirdly, it split the Hungarian nation in two. As long as the rebellion was a contract between the nobility and the serfs (who formed the majority of the population), most Hungarians were united behind it since they believed a rebel victory would improve their lot. By killing two of their own kind, it became clear to the serfs that Rákóczi was merely a front for a faction of self-serving nobles. In short, the assembly at Onod cost Rákóczi popular support.

The economic situation remained dire. In September 1707, treasury employees in Solivar rebelled after not being paid for seven weeks. The miners of Banska and Smolne continued their strike. Rákóczi despatched troops under Colonel Neumann to Banska in September to suppress the strikers. In a violent encounter, eleven were killed.

Even so, Rákóczi still controlled most of Upper Hungary and the Great Plain, with Transdanubia and Transylvania changing hands with a monotonous regularity. From this position of relative strength, he now planned to invade Bohemia and Moravia, in order to get closer to the Rhine, where France and Bavaria might come to his assistance. Confronted

Peter Zrinyi's castle at Osalj

Nikolai Zrinyi's castle at Cakovec

Rákóczi Castle at Zborov

Bardejov market square

The fortress of Mukachevo

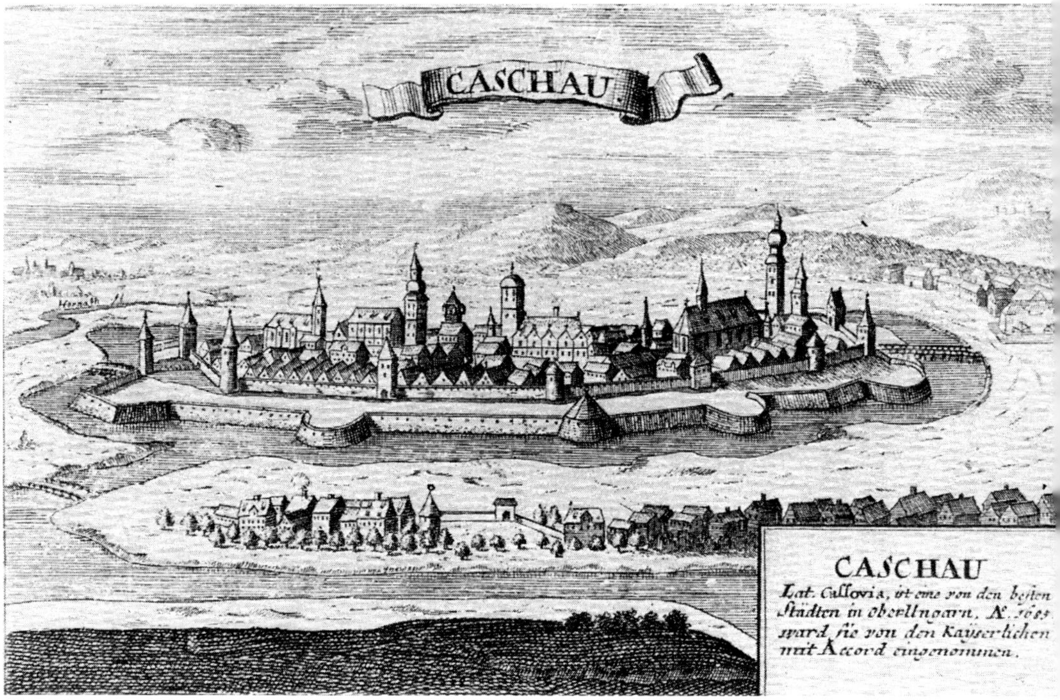

Košice

St. Elizabeth's cathedral in Košice

Sárospatak Castle

Borša manor house

Sieniawaska Castle at Berezhany

Rákóczi castle at Tokay

Trencín Castle

Trnava

by the departure of Starhemberg for Spain and with General Rabutin being too ill to campaign, the Emperor Joseph reinstated General Heister in 1708 and despatched him with 7,400 men to close with Rákóczi's force of 14,000 outside Trencín. It was to be a turning point.

As Generals Heister and Pálffy marched from Bratislava and General Vird from Moravia into Upper Hungary, Rákóczi's lieutenants urged him to protect his rear, advising him to capture the castle at Trencín before venturing north. When Heister arrived in the area, he found the *kuruc* forces dug in on the forward slopes of the mountains to the east of Trencín, overlooking the Váh valley and the fortress. On the right flank, he could make out the *kuruc* light horse with part of the infantry under the command of General Pekry. More infantry occupied the wooded country close to the village of Hamre, which was interwoven with trenches. The centre of the *kuruc* position, held by German and Polish carabineers in Rákóczi's service, shielded the artillery commanded by the French General De Le Mothe. Heister concluded that the *kuruc* position was unassailable and started to withdraw towards Trencín to seek the protection offered by the long-range guns of its fortress.

As Heister organised his troops for a withdrawal, Rákóczi gave the command to open fire and ordered Pekry to attack the rearguard of the Imperial forces with his light cavalry. The ground however was far from suited to a cavalry charge since it was flanked by two large ponds and dissected by a narrow dyke. When Pekry realised it would be difficult to withdraw should his attack prove unsuccessful, he gave the order to fall back, a move that quickly degenerated into chaos. Pálffy, having watched the ensuing confusion, counter-attacked with the seasoned Eszterházy and Nádasdy regiments of Hussars. The *kurucs* in the vicinity panicked and fled. Meanwhile the overall battle had begun in earnest, but the dire plight of the cavalry on the right flank infected morale across the rest of the *kuruc* front. Riding from sector to sector, Rákóczi tried to encourage his soldiers to remain calm and disciplined but he was unsaddled. He recounts in his memoirs how his horse "had already jumped over two ditches, but the third one was too close; it missed its footing, made a somersault and dropped down stone dead. My good luck was to be thrown off to one side but I received a great blow to my left eye, which made me lose consciousness."

Rumours of his death caused his units to panic and they fled from the field of battle. In less than three hours, Heister's force had managed to shatter a *kuruc* army nearly three times its size. The *kurucs* left behind 3,000 dead, including General De La Mothe. The victors captured 500 prisoners and all the *kuruc* artillery against a loss of around 160 of their own men.

Rákóczi and Bercsényi retreated in good order to Topolcany and then to Nitranska Streda. After this victory, Nitra fell to the Imperial forces and Heister occupied the whole north-west sector of Hungary with only the fortress of Nové Zámky resisting. More importantly, the *kuruc* spirit began to evaporate. In the past, the re-conquered territories had risen up as soon as the Imperial army had left, but when that December, Rákóczi called his faithful followers to arms, few answered. His promises to free peasants from their lords in return for military service, made the previous month at the Diet of Sárospatak, had not been believed. The Austrians could now begin to pacify Hungary in earnest.

Disaffection set in among Rákóczi's commanders: Brigadier Ocskay, later executed by a *kuruc* unit, and Bezeredy both defected in the autumn of 1708. In September 1709 the irrepressible van Bottyan died, while the plague swept through Hungary; seven years of war had killed 85,000 men and seven months of plague over 400,000 people. Forced into a small corner of Northern Hungary, where 'villages were without inhabitants and in every bush there lay the corpse of a soldier', Rákóczi took stock of his situation. On the one hand, he thought it fair to say that 'the *Kuruc* army was not defeated by the Emperor, who had sent 13 generals and three regular armies; Austria did not win a single battle; famine, fatigue and the plague defeated the struggle for freedom.' On the other, he failed to win the crucial major battle against the Habsburgs which would have forced them to the negotiating table out of weakness rather than strength.

For Rákóczi's principal benefactor, Louis XIV, the years 1709 to 1711 were disastrous. The winter of 1709, the worst for a hundred years when the temperature in Paris fell to minus 20 degrees Centigrade, decimated half France's livestock as well as blighting the olive, walnut and wine harvests. "Children live on boiled grass and roots," wrote the Attorney-General of the Parliament of Burgundy. "Some even crop the fields like sheep." Louis tried to sue for peace but the Allies' terms were too onerous. In September

1710, Marlborough and Prince Eugene inflicted a crushing defeat on the French army at Malplaquet. With his army shattered, his people hungry and peace denied except on intolerable terms, Louis had no choice other than to relegate Hungary to the bottom of his list of strategic priorities. Then personal tragedy followed; three Dauphins died in the space of a year as well as Louis' beloved granddaughter Marie Adelaide.

Still seeking an international diplomatic solution, despite the intransigence of the Habsburgs, Rákóczi now increased his efforts to turn the Hungarian rebellion into a European issue through the despatch of envoys to peace conferences in 1709 and 1710, and letters to Queen Anne and representatives of the various Protestant churches. His proposal to renounce his princely title if Transylvania's sovereignty and independence were guaranteed was well received by Marlborough. He trusted Rákóczi and liked the idea of Transylvania as the pivot for the balance of power in Europe.

Rákóczi, desperately trying to raise the siege of Nové Zámky, was defeated by Pálffy at Romhany on 22 January 1710. The 2,000 Polish, Lithuanian and Swedish troops, who had joined Rákóczi after the disastrous defeat of Charles XII at Poltava the previous June, now abandoned him. From now on, Rákóczi no longer constituted a military threat to the Emperor and to all extents was defeated. Nine months later, on 24 September, the Austrians finally captured Nové Zámky. At the end of the year the fortified towns of Bardejov and Presov also fell. In the rest of Hungary the Imperial army also made major advances. This left only Košice, Uzhgorod, Mukachevo and Chust in *kuruc* hands.

Despite his high personal standing in the courts of Europe, Rákóczi was isolated and at his wits' end. At his castle at Sárospatak, he watched the carts and carriages of the Transylvanian nobility pass by, full of emaciated children and starving women who assured him with tears in their eyes that their husbands would be faithful to him unto death. Almost the whole country was in flight. In his *Confessions of a Sinner*, Rákóczi wrote: "Winter raged, and enormous masses of snow covered the ground, so that even horsemen could only use the roads: the fleeing masses with their loaded peasant carts wandered from village to village, searching partly for sustenance and partly for security in the mountains and hiding places in the marshes. Soldiers deserted the flag in order to save and feed their families, and the sorrowful lament of the people and refugees constantly sounded in my ears....they had not given up soldiering because of disloyalty or ill-will but because the situation had become intolerable....I was distressed not at having to leave the country or by exile from my homeland, but because I had not safeguarded the lives of any of them."

Having met with General Pállfy, the Emperor's representative, on 31 January 1711, Rákóczi was unable to concede anything of importance and three weeks later he left Mukachevo for the last time, heading for a meeting with Peter the Great in Poland. Before departing, he gave Sándor Károlyi permission to enter into peace negotiations with Pállfy. Despite the sudden death of Joseph I from smallpox on 17 April, the opportunity for Károlyi to negotiate with Pállfy, a fellow Hungarian, was too good to be missed. The Treaty of Szatmár (Satu Mare) went ahead and was signed two weeks later by Károlyi and 151 Hungarian dignitaries. In Barcelona, the Emperor's heir, his brother Charles VI, made conciliatory noises, admitting that the tranquillity of the Hungarians was a vital interest of Austria.

On the plain of Majteny, near Satu Mare, the remaining 13,000 members of the *kuruc* army laid down their tattered regimental colours to the wail of the *tárogatós*. The vision of unconditional freedom for Hungary, which had guided both Thököly and Rákóczi, remained as elusive as ever. Without sufficient professional military forces, adequate money and international support, defeat was inevitable.

The terms of the treaty were astonishingly mild: a general amnesty for all, including Rákóczi, who would also regain his estates if he swore an oath of allegiance to the Emperor; the promise of religious freedom albeit with no external guarantees; respect for the constitution and the convocation of the Diet to discuss matters further; the peasants' privileges granted by Rákóczi were to be left intact and all foreign administrative posts such as the *Neoacquistica Commissio* were to be eliminated. These were entirely different to the terms dictated nearly a century before to Bohemia and Moravia, and in many respects represented a considerable political victory for Rákóczi.

Rákóczi's reply was short and to the point: "The price of (this) peace is liberty". He refused to sign and thus forfeited all his estates. Sárospatak was summarily given to Prince Trautsohn. What did he mean by this succinct rebuttal? Modern commentators see in the Treaty of Szatmár an unacceptable compromise between the Estates and the Habsburg dynasty based on the status quo ante—'ossification' as one put it—at the expense of the political and social freedoms Rákóczi wanted for all levels of society. Certainly, the peasant masses who had started the revolt with Rákóczi, gained nothing from the peace. Indeed, if anything, they were worse off in what came to be called 'the second serfdom' and he never forgave Károlyi who he considered a traitor from then on. But there is no question that Rákóczi fundamentally found the terms without guarantees unacceptable; if the Hungarians had learned one thing over the last hundred years, it was that Vienna could not be trusted.

At this point, Peter the Great reappeared on the scene and met with Rákóczi at Yavorov near L'vov on 12 May. Bolstered by his dramatic victory over the Swedish king at Poltava, the Tsar promised to come to Rákóczi's aid just as soon as he had seen off the Turks in Moldavia. Unfortunately, this was not to happen. The Turks defeated the Russians on 9 July at the battle of the Prut River and Peter retreated to his home base at St. Petersburg.

After nearly two years in Poland hoping for a change in the direction of the political wind, Rákóczi now chose exile. "If I go into exile, hope remains with me, because I will preserve my people's affection, which will live in my people's hearts forever until my last breath." Still confident that the independence of the Principality of Transylvania might be included in the imminent peace treaties, he sailed from Danzig on 20 November 1712 in a small English ship sent by Queen Anne. He reached Dieppe after a hazardous voyage on 13 January and made his way to Versailles where Louis received him warmly. Much sought after by ladies of the court, including Madame Maintenon and Louise-Bénédicte, the dangerous Duchesse of Maine, and befriended by the Count of Toulouse and the Dukes of Villeroy and Sully, Rákóczi soon became a familiar figure in the salons of Versailles. The King presented him with a hunting box at Rambouillet and a suite of rooms at the royal castle of Marly. But there was no independence for Transylvania on the agenda at the Treaty of Utrecht (1713) or Rastatt (1714). Rákóczi's choice of János Klement, who styled himself a secret agent, as his representative to these conferences was ill-advised.

On Louis's death on 1 September 1715, Rákóczi found himself out of favour at court and took up residence in a Camaldolese monastery outside Paris, where he led a quiet life aside from an affectionate meeting with Peter the Great in Paris in 1717. Kelemen Mikes, Rákóczi's chamberlain, wryly observed: "But among princes blood-ties and friendship are like a reed; when you prosper, both blood-ties and friendship are exalted; but when it goes badly with you and you look to them for help, all they say is: *nescio vos*." The door to Versailles was locked and the Duc d'Orleans and the Duc du Maine had no intention of readmitting Rákóczi to its mirrored halls.

Meanwhile, in January 1715, Sultan Ahmet III's new belligerent Sadrazam, Damad Ali, had attacked Venice. After a three week siege, Corinth fell to the Ottomans and the gates to the Morea were opened. The Porte had tentatively asked Vienna to remain neutral and had taken for granted that Austria would remain on the sidelines. This was a serious miscalculation and when the Venetians invoked the emperor's support on the grounds that the Treaty of Karlowitz had been violated, Charles VI declared war on the Porte. The outcome was by no means a foregone conclusion; the Turks mustered some 150,000 men against the Imperial forces of 125,000. The exiled *kurucs* took heart, believing that here was one final chance to wrest independence from Vienna. Bercsényi sent a small number of trusted men to Hungary to make preparations for an insurrection and renew the *kuruc* confederation.

In 1716, Rákóczi received an unexpected letter in a silver envelope with a gold seal. It was from Sultan Ahmet III, inviting him to join the new Ottoman offensive as a confederate: if they were successful, Transylvania would be his. He left for Edirne but it was too late: the Turkish army had already been defeated by Prince Eugene and General Pálffy at Peterwardein on 5 August. Prince Eugene followed his success by capturing Timisoara, the last surviving bulwark of Islam in Hungary, signalling the end of Ottoman rule in the Banat.

In their indomitable fashion, the *kurucs* continued as if nothing had changed. Bercsényi marched his troops, who now numbered about 1,000, to link up with the main Ottoman army at Belgrade, where in June 1717 they once more faced the massed forces of Prince Eugene. In a typically daring move, Eugene's infantry charged the Janissaries with fixed bayonets; the whole Ottoman line broke up in disorder and fled. Then Count Antal Eszterházy appeared on the borders of Transylvania on 22 August with a motley force of Ottoman mercenaries. Instead of attacking the Imperial army, he marched his men in two columns towards Cluj and the Tisza River, "plundering, looting, settings things on fire and carrying off the population". Far from being a popular uprising, this ill-conceived sally was dubbed 'the last Mongol invasion'. It was finally seen off by local Hungarian levies under the command of the former *kuruc* hero, Count Sándor Károlyi.

The Turks, however, did not withdraw their offer of hospitality to Rákóczi, who had sailed from Marseilles on board the L'Ange Gabriel and arrived in Gallipoli in October 1717. After the Peace of Passarowitz in July the following year, when the Porte gave up the rest of Hungary, most of Serbia and part of Wallachia and Bosnia, the French ambassador to the Porte informed Rákóczi that with effect from 2 August, the French, Dutch, English and Austrian authorities had agreed to ban from their territories any person considered seditious. In effect, the *kuruc* leaders were forbidden to visit Western Europe. Furthermore, on Austrian insistence, Rákóczi and his entourage, including Bercsényi and Forgách, were installed first at Yeniköy and then, on 24 April 1720, at Tekirdağ on the European shore of the Sea of Marmara.

Then came an unexpected financial set back. In April 1713, Louis had given Rákóczi 600,000 livres tournois in compensation for his loyalty to France in the form of bonds of 'l'hotel de ville de Paris'. For convenience, Rákóczi registered them in the name of his secretary and agent, Domokos Brenner, who had loyally served him since 1705. On arrival in Tekirdag, Rákóczi discovered that without his permission Brenner had exchanged the bonds for shares in the bank of John Law, which subsequently folded. This led to Brenner's arrest for embezzlement on 24 September 1721; he committed suicide in the Bastille three days later. His property was disposed of by the state, his creditors paid off and the balance given to the upkeep of the prison. Not a sou found its way back to Rákóczi.

During the next 15 years at Tekirdağ, Rákóczi spent much of his life following a monastic regime. Kelemen Mikes recorded the daily routine: "at half past five in the morning the drum is beaten, then the servants must rise and be ready for six o'clock. There is a drum-call at six, and the Prince dresses—then he goes to Chapel and hears Mass. After Mass, he goes to the dining hall, where we drink coffee and smoke. When it is a quarter to eight the first drum is beaten for Mass, and at eight o'clock the second, and the third a little later—then the Prince goes to Mass, and after Mass he goes to his own house and everyone may go where he pleases. At half-past eleven the drum beats for luncheon and at twelve we sit down and do justice to the chickens. At half past two the Prince goes alone to the Chapel, and remains there until three. When it is a quarter to five the first drum sounds for evening prayer, the second at five o'clock and the third a little later—then the Prince goes to the Chapel and afterwards everyone goes their way. The drum for dinner is beaten at half past seven. Dinner does not last long, and at eight o'clock the Prince undresses, but most often does not yet go to bed at that hour...."

If he had hoped for a diplomatic role in Istanbul, it was not to be. With the appointment of Nevsehirli Ibrahim Paşa as Sadrazam in 1717, the thirteenth incumbent in as many years, an era of stability began, allowing the Sultan to concentrate on his favourite pastime, the production of tulips. When his envoy returned from Paris in 1720 with descriptions of the parterres at Versailles, Ahmet III embarked on a gardening frenzy and soon flower gardens and avenues of trees sprung up all over the summer palace at Sa'adabad, which was modelled on the Chateau du Marly. When he was not gardening or siring children, Ahmet III was throwing extravagant parties, known as *helva* fetes: it took the French ambassador eight months to obtain an audience with the fun-loving ruler.

In September 1730, the party came to an abrupt end: an Albanian ex-soldier, Patrona Halil, began a popular revolt against these "Frankish manners", forcing Ahmet first to appease him with the dead bodies of his Sadrazam and other advisers, and then to resign in favour of his nephew Mahmut I. Patrona Halil still held sway with the populace, but Mahmut ousted him with an invitation to the Topkapi on the pretence of appointing him a general. Led by the new Sadrazam, a murderous ambush followed, leaving Halil and his Albanian bodyguard dead. Over 7,000 of his followers were killed on the streets of the city during the next three days. In less than a year, another revolt broke out led by another Albanian, Kara Ali. This was quickly put down with the initial elimination of 400 rebels; however, the purges that followed ended with a final count of 10,000 executions in ten days. After this, Mahmut had no further problems with his subjects until his death in 1754. Throughout these turbulent events, Rákóczi remained isolated at Tekirdağ.

In 1733, after the death of Augustus II of Saxony, King of Poland, the Russian Tsarina Anna joined forces with Vienna in a war against France and Spain for the spoils of the Polish succession; while they pressed the Porte to remain neutral, France lobbied for Turkish intervention. The Porte demanded a formal alliance with Paris which was rejected after much debate; the idea of an overt formal alliance between Christian and Islamic states was never a runner. Taking advantage of these protracted negotiations, the Russians advanced to Danzig, installed their candidate, Augustus III, on the Polish throne in Warsaw and then sent their army south to Azov, which fell on 19 June 1736. Unable to intervene or influence, Rákóczi watched these events from afar,

It was not a happy outcome to a life which had once shone so brightly. There was also a heavy personal price to pay: retired to a convent in Saint Germain, his wife, Amalie, died in Paris in February 1722, aged 43. Of their four children, two sons survived and in June 1727, the youngest, 26-year-old György, arrived from Vienna to meet his father for the first time. Rákóczi was overjoyed but after experiencing ten months of boredom and poor health, György left for France the following March leaving his father desolate. A year later, Princess Sieniawska, Rákóczi's lover and confidante from the time of his first exile in Poland, passed away, leaving few living links to his past. His mentor, comrade-in-arms and friend, Bercsényi, had died in Tekirdağ in November 1725.

At three in the morning of Good Friday 1735, the last Prince of Transylvania died peacefully at the age of 60. His organs were buried in a casket in the local Greek church and his heart was sent to the monastery at Gros Bois in France, according to his wishes. His body was despatched to the Jesuits in Istanbul, where "they dug a grave on the spot where our lord's mother (Helena Thököly) had been buried. Only her skull was found, and that was placed in her son's coffin, and they were buried together." His elder son, Jozsef, arrived to administer his father's estate in December 1736. Within two years he was dead, struck down by a fever on the Danube. The Sultan refused permission for him to be buried next to his father and he was laid to rest in the little Greek church at Csernavoda.

The Discontented: Love, War and Betrayal

In October 1904, with the permission of the Emperor Franz-Joseph and the Sultan, the remains of Rákóczi, his mother and his son Jozsef, together with those of Counts Antal Eszterházy and Miklós Bercsényi were retrieved from Turkey. Two years later their funeral took place in great splendour in St Stephan's Cathedral in Budapest. They were finally laid to rest in a tomb at St Elizabeth's cathedral in Košice on 29 October 1906.

In summing up the life of Ferenc Rákóczi, one has first to recognise his undoubted brilliance. Fluent in six languages, he was a gifted orator, an able politician and polished diplomat. As a competent soldier and talented administrator, he created an 80,000 strong army and kept it operational in the field for eight years. His commitment to the cause of Hungarian independence was unconditional and indisputable. The sheer scale of his achievement is breathtaking in the context of early 18th century Europe: commander-in-chief, foreign minister, treasurer, battlefield general, minister of armaments, he was virtually a one-man government, fulfilling each role with distinction.

Above all, Rákóczi was a realist. From the beginning he recognised his weaknesses in both military and financial matters, and took decisive steps to mitigate them. As the heir to Thököly's swashbuckling guerrilla army, he knew that securing political and financial independence from the Habsburgs would be possible only from a position of overwhelming international strength derived from military supremacy on the battlefield. But therein lays the contradiction in his character. For only a romantic, and an optimistic one at that, could have envisaged the destruction of the Habsburg military machine by an amateur Hungarian army, however brave.

It was to take over one hundred and thirty years before another Hungarian army took to the field against the Habsburgs. A further nineteen years passed before a compromise—*The Ausgleich*—was eventually reached in 1867. Even then, the man who was crowned King of Hungary at the Church of Matthias in Buda was none other than Emperor Franz-Joseph. When independence finally came in 1920, the price demanded by the Allies at Trianon was 70% of its pre-war territories but at least the ghosts of Zrinyi's Hungarian heroes could finally sleep.

Sources Consulted

Account of the Turks Wars: Le Croy, Paris 1711.

Acktenstucke auf Geschichte Franz Rákóczi's und seiner Verbindungen mit dem Auslande: edited by Joseph Fiedler.

Amours of Count Teckeli and the Lady Aurora Veronica de Serini: Russell Street, Covent Garden 1686.

Austria's Eastern Question 1700–1790: Karl Roider, Princeton University Press 1982.

Borderland—a Journey through the History of the Ukraine: Anna Reid, Phoenix 2003.

Caraffa és az Eperjesi vér Törvnyszék: K.Papp Miklós, Pest 1863.

Conduct and character of Count Nicholas Serini: London 1664.

Danube: Claudio Magris, Harvill Press 2001.

Erdély röved története: Akadémia Kiadó, Budapest 1989.

Etudes sur Francois 11 Rákóczi, Prince de Transylvanie: Emile Pillias, Librairie Ernest Leroux, Paris 1939.

Five Hungarian Writers: D. Mervyn Jones, Clarendon 1966.

From Hunyadi to Rákóczi—War and Society in late Medieval and Early Modern Hungary: edited by János Bak and Béla Kiraly

George Stepney: Correspondence wit Robert Harley 1704–7, with the Duke of Marlborough 1702–7, with Lord Sunderland 1705–7, with Charles Whitworth 1702–6, with Adam Cardonnel 1704–6; British Library.

George Stepney: Memoranda books June 1704–August 1705, August 1705–February 1706, February 1706–January 1707; National Archives.

Habsburg Monarchy 1490–1848—attributes of Empire: Paula Sutter Fichter, Palgrave Macmillan 2003.

Habsburg Monarchy: Charles Ingrao, Cambridge University Press 2000.

Habsburgs: Andrew Wheatcroft, Viking 1995.

Habsburgs: Edward Crankshaw, Weidenfeld and Nicolson 1971.

Histoire d'Emeric, Comte de Tekeli pour server a sa vie: Jean Le Clerc 1693.

Histoire des Revolutions de Hongrie: anon, A La Haye chez Jean Neaulme 1739.

Histoire du Princ Ragotzi ou La Guerre des Mecontens sous son Commandement: A.Cassovie 1707.

Histoire Interessante ou Relation des guerres du Nord et de Hongris: Marquis de Bonnac 1756.

History of modern Europe—from the Capture of Constantinople 1453 to the Treaty of Berlin 1878: Prof Sir Richard Lodge, John Murray, 1906.

History of Romania: Kurt Treptow, Centre for Romanian Studies 2000.

History of the Habsburg Empire 1273–1700: Jean Bérenger, Pearson Education 2002.

History of the Habsburg Empire 1700–1918: Jean Bérenger, Pearson Education 2002.

History of the Habsburg Empire 1526–1918: Robert Kahn, University of California Press 1974.

History of the Protestant Church in Hungary: James Nisbet 1854.

History of the Roumanians: R.W.Seton-Watson. Cambridge University Press 1934.

Hungarian Heroes of Liberty: Julia de Eőrsi, Budapest 1929.

Hungarian Rebellion: William Gilbert, London 1672.

Hungarians: Paul Lendvai, Hurst 1999.

Hungary, a short history: Aldine, Chicago 1962.

Inside the Seraglio: John Freely, Viking 1999.

Sources Consulted

Leopold I of Austria: John Speilman, Thames and Hudson 1977.

Les Memoires du Prince Francois Rákóczi sur la guerre de Hongrie.

Letters from Turkey: Kelemen Mikes, Keegan Paul International 2000.

Louis XIV: Vincent Cronin, Harvill 1996.

Making of the Habsburg Monarchy 1550–1700: R.J.W. Evans, Clarendon Press 1979.

Memoires de Montecuculi: 1770.

Memoirs of Miklos Bethlen.

Millenium in Central Europe—a history of Hungary: László Kontler, Atlantisz Könyvkiadó, Budapest 1999.

Millennium of Hungarian Military History: Veszprémy and Király, Atlantic Research & Publications Inc 2002.

Munkácstól Rodostóig II Rákoczi F. Elete: Dr. Schöner Ferenc, Budapest 1914.

Osman's Dream: Caroline Finkel, John Murray 2005.

Ottoman Centuries: Lord Kinross, Perennial 2002.

Ottomans: Andrew Wheatcroft, Penguin 1995.

Peter the Great—a biography: Lindsey Hughes, Yale University Press 2004.

Prince Eugene of Savoy: G.B.Malleson, Chapman & Hall 1885.

Prince Eugen of Savoy: Nicholas Henderson, London 1964.

Prince Eugene of Savoy: Derek McKay, London 1977.

Quest for the Miracle Stag: Tertia 2000.

Question of Empire—Leopold I and the War of the Spanish Succession 1701–1705: Linda and Marshal Frey, East European Monographs 1983.

Rákóczi Ferenc II: Köpeczi Béla and Várkonyi Agnes, Gondolat, Budapest 1976.

Rákóczi Ferenc-Bujdosáasa (1710–1712): Szalay László, Pest 1864.

Relatione della Resa dell' Importante Fortezzadi Mongatsch: Bologna 1688.

Rise of the Habsburg Empire 1526–1815: Victor Mamatey, Holt, Rinehart and Winston 1971.

Sárospatak: Mihály Détshy, Pëtofi Printing House 1970.

Secret history of the Austrian Government: A.Michiels, Chapman & Hall 1859

The Eastern Question—An Historical Study of European Diplomacy: Sir J.A.R. Marriott, Clarendon Press 1919.

Transylvania: István Lázár, Simon Publications 1997.

Treaties of the War of the Spanish Succession—An Historical and Critical Dictionary.

Venetian Empire: Jan Morris, Penguin 1990.

Zrinyi Helena: Horvath Mihály, Pest 1869

Locations Visited

Croatia
Ozalj
Čakovec
Zagreb

Hungary
Boldogkő
Budapest
Eger
Esztergom
Füzér
Füzérradvány
Miskolc
Regéc
Sárospatak
Sopron
Tokaj
Vác

Slovakia
Bardejov
Borša
Kežmarok
Košice
Muráň
Nitra
Oravsky Hrad

THE DISCONTENTED: LOVE, WAR AND BETRAYAL

Presov
Strečno
Trenčín
Trnava
Váh Valley
Zborov

Romania
Cluj
Iernut
Jibou
Oradea
Satu Mare
Sibiu
Zărneşti

Ukraine
Mukachevo
Turkey
Tekirdağ